Praise for *Bars, Dumps & Other Childhood Hangouts*

Everyone involved in foster care should read this first-hand account. It illuminates what goes on inside a good kid handed a difficult life through no fault of her own. The profound change foster care parents can make in a child's life is also shown, but the book's greatest impact will be in regards to enabling understanding the things foster kids may not be able to say on their own behalf. A touching story that has the potential to change lives for the better.

Stephanie Grace Whitson
Award-winning, best-selling novelist

As a child, all Kathy wanted was safety, protection, and comfort—was that too much to ask? While some grown-ups were helpful, others looked the other way. Most grown-ups were a perplexing combination of good and bad. In her book, Kathy poignantly portrays a little girl growing up in an environment that threatened to snuff the life out of her. Through it all, she showed remarkable resilience that finally led her to that place of safety that she so deserved. Grown-ups everywhere—in churches, in neighborhoods, in schools, in professionals' offices—need to step up and speak out for the Kathys in their world.

Jeanette Harder PhD.
Professor, Grace Abbott School of Social Work, University of Nebraska – Omaha
Co-Founder, Dove's Nest
Author of *Let the Children Come: Preparing Faith Communities to End Child Abuse and Neglect*

Published by Workplay Publishing
Newton, KS 67114

workplaypublishing.com

Copyright © 2013, 2020 Katherine Burkey Wiens. All rights reserved.

Original cover design by Jim L. Friesen. Interior layout by André Swartley.

ISBN 978-0-9911405-1-0

PRINTED IN THE UNITED STATES OF AMERICA

BARS DUMPS & OTHER
Childhood Hangouts

a memoir by
Katherine Burkey Wiens

Workplay Publishing

Contents

Foreword	9
Prologue	11
Death and Redemption	17
Opening Presents Before Christmas	29
Ulysses	35
The Condemned House	39
Sacred Heart	46
The Hunger in My Life	50
The Day Frank Died	59
Trauma and Aftermath of Death	66
The End Starts Here	73
Unsafe Environments	80
Running Away	87
Alone with Josephine	92
God, I Need a Miracle	99
The Day Pat Came Back	106
Where has Josephine Gone	110
Walking around the Block	113
Leaving My Life	120
Cedars Children's Home	128
They Wanted a Little Girl	133
My New Life	141
My New Family	145
Epilogue	159

In loving memory of Floyd and Erma Burkey
my real parents and earthly saviors.
To Tim,
my safe place.
To little Kathy,
whose strength and courage made it possible
for me to be who I am today.

FOREWORD

For several reasons I wanted this story told. The main reason is because no one has known me my entire life—no immediate family member, extended family, or friend.

This story is about the first ten years of my life. After I was taken away from my biological family at age ten I had very little contact with any of them until I was in my thirties. My foster/adoptive family knew some of what happened to me but were not given a lot of details. This book will bring my story full circle, connecting the woman I am today with the little girl of my past.

My initial reason for writing the book was to tell this story, but as I got into the writing process, another need for this book became evident. As my writing coach, Laurie Oswald Robinson, began reading the stories of my childhood, she helped me see how others, who had not experienced this kind of life, could gain a deeper understanding of childhood poverty and abuse. I hope this story will help teachers, foster parents, counselors, and anyone else who works with children experiencing poverty, abuse, and neglect or who are in the foster care system.

There are questions of identity this book does not fully explain. Identity has been an issue throughout my life: Who am I and where do I belong? The biggest question is: Who is my biological father? This is a question that remains unanswered for me although a family member has given me a lead to who the person may be. I have not investigated this yet.

The other question is that of adoption by my foster family. I was never legally adopted. They wanted to adopt me when I was a child, but my biological mother would not give up her parental rights. For me (and for them) the Burkey family is my family. My parents chose me to be their child. I did not come to them through the natural birthing process, but they chose and wanted me to be a part of their family.

The last issue I will cover is sexual abuse. Because I do not go into great detail, some readers may question the abuse, asking if the abuse I suffered was criminal. The legal term for what I experienced as a child is "aggravated indecent liberties with a child." There were many more situations where I was sexually abused by family members or family friends in my first ten years. For personal reasons I chose to reveal only a few situations in this book. After I was taken away from my biological family all sexual abuse ended.

In writing this book, I choose to honor the memories of the little girl. I did not do a lot of research or interviews with family members. I used my early memories and wove a story around them. This is little Kathy's story.

PROLOGUE

Hope can come in the midst of desperation, and tragedy can give rise to miracles. Desperation and tragedy defined my birth mother's life. She struggled with poverty, alcoholism, troubled relationships, the loss of loved ones, and a lack of skills and resources.

But hope often comes from new life, from the birth of a child. My story with my birth mother began in Lincoln, Nebraska. She was forty years old and about to give birth for the third time.

She and my stepfather separated for several months. They reunited before my birth, but, more importantly, they had been separated when I was conceived.

Josephine Clara Mahoney Shorny knew the child that was about to burst from her body was not her husband's. Everyone knew it. They all knew her husband, Frank, was not my father because she got pregnant when they were separated and he was sterile.

As a teenager, he was sent to a mental hospital where he was

Josephine and baby Kathy

sterilized. In the 1920s and 1930s, sterilizations were routinely performed on those admitted to state mental institutions.

Josephine's family—her mother, three sisters and one brother—also knew this child was not Frank's. Josephine, the oldest child of William and Clara Mahoney, believed that her parents loved her, but she knew the rest of her family and Frank's family disapproved of her. Josephine's sisters, who had made their own way in the world, felt she was taking advantage of their parents. Even at age forty, she needed help from her parents because, once again, she had gotten pregnant. They wondered if Josephine even knew who the baby's father was. If she did, she certainly didn't tell any of them.

Scorn also came from Frank's mother, Antonia. She was an immigrant from Czechoslovakia and loved her two boys, Ernest and the younger Frank. She knew Frank was not perfect, but she had convinced herself that most of his problem were due to Josephine's bad influence and not because of the many poor choices he had made. Josephine knew Frank's mother hated her just for being in his life. Now she had embarrassed them further by getting pregnant again while he was away. Would Antonia even care that she was having a baby? Would she hate this baby, too?

Beyond the scorn, lies, and denial, the beautiful truth was a new life would soon be coming into this world. My journey with my mother was about to begin. Perhaps that day went something like this. Josephine felt the first agonizing pains of labor early in the morning. As Frank lay sleeping, she got up and went straight to the refrigerator. She felt guilty about drinking so early in the morning, but the pain was becoming unbearable, and she needed relief. When she opened the refrigerator door, a cool wave of air flowed over her. She reached for a bottle of beer, expecting to take only a couple of swallows to help with the pain. Instead, she drank until the bottle was empty. She put it in the trash, so Frank would not see it.

In 1959, no one talked about the damaging effects alcohol could have on a developing baby, but if Frank saw her with the beer so early in the morning, he might accuse her of being a drunk. In truth, however, she didn't care. She just needed a little drink to take the edge off and help her feel better. After all, it wasn't like she was drinking hard liquor like whisky or vodka at seven in the morning.

She used the bathroom and looked at her reflection in the mirror as she washed her hands. Curly, brown hair hung down to her shoulders. It was wild from sleep and wiry from the home permanents her mother and sisters had given her. She had large brown eyes and a huge nose. Her face was puffy from the pregnancy. Soon it would be over, and that would be a relief.

She walked back to bed, her huge stomach stuck out in front and its skin stretched tight. When she lay back down, the two other times she had given birth flooded her memory.

The first time her mother was there to help. It was a long

and hard birth. When the baby finally came, she sensed something was wrong. The nurse quickly took it. When she and the doctor came back into the room, Josephine was thrilled at the hope of seeing her new baby. Instead of joy, she received painful news. The baby was dead. The cord had wrapped around his neck, and he suffocated during birth. The nurse brought the baby into the room, and Josephine held him. Tears rolled down her checks as she stared at the lifeless body. Gone were her dreams about being a mother and about loving and being loved by this child. She named the baby William, after her father.

Now, ten years later, lying in bed on this hot August morning, tears trickled down Josephine's face into her ears. The sorrow and guilt of that first birth remained sharp in her memory. Perhaps God had punished her for getting pregnant when she wasn't married.

To calm her from this painful memory, she reached over to the bed stand and took a cigarette from the package. After lighting it, she pulled hard on it to suck in the smoke. As the nicotine entered her body, she felt better. She grabbed the large glass ashtray, balancing it on her stomach as she remembered the other birth she had experienced.

Her little boy, Patrick, born on St. Patrick's Day, was now seven. The nuns at the Catholic hospital and her family had insisted she name him Patrick. Born healthy, he later developed a sunken chest and was slow in school. She and Frank were married by then, and Frank loved and accepted Patrick as his son.

Would Frank accept this baby as well? Would it be a healthy child? It moved and kicked a lot. The few times she had gone to the doctor, he had told her everything was fine.

Now her body was telling her again it was time to pee. As she strained to get out of bed, she felt a burst of water rush between her legs. It created a puddle on the floor. Her water had broken; the baby was coming.

She phoned her mother and then Dona, her sister-inlaw. Even though Josephine had three sisters, she felt most comfortable with Dona, who had married, but divorced, Josephine's brother, also named Frank. Dona did not judge Josephine as harshly as her sisters did. In addition, Dona always seemed willing to help. She was smart and strong, not timid and weak like Josephine. Dona knew how to handle situations and was not afraid to tell people exactly what she thought.

After Josephine's call to Dona, she let Frank know about the baby's soon arrival. They woke Patrick and drove to the hospital.

My birth certificate says I was born August 23, 1959, to Josephine and Frank Shorny. I never questioned the fact that Frank was my father until I was an adult and married with young children. Even today, in my fifties, the identity of my biological father remains a mystery.

However, on the day of my birth, Josephine worried about Frank's reaction. When he came into the room and saw me, he smiled. Since he was a man of few words, his silence did not bother Josephine. On the contrary, she was overjoyed that he seemed happy with their new daughter.

"I want to name her Frantislea, after my great-grandmother from Austria," Josephine said. "We can call her 'Fran.'" She had chosen that name because she admired her great-grandmother, at least from all the stories she had heard and her childhood memories about this woman. Also, Josephine wanted to give me a name that was not Irish. Her father was half Irish and proud of it. But Frank and her father did not get along. What's more, "Frantislea" sounded like "Frank." Maybe that would help him feel more like the child was his.

However, Frank would not agree to that name. He said Frantislea was too long, and he couldn't pronounce it. So Josephine gave him her second choice. "Let's call her Katherine.

That's a good Czech name and my grandmother's middle name." She paused and waited for Frank's reaction, but when he gave none, she continued, "We could call her Kathy. That would be easy to remember and pronounce."

Frank's silence continued. Josephine waited, hoping he would agree and there would not be a fight. Finally, he said, "That sounds good," and he walked out of the room. For the first eighteen years of my life I was Katherine Josephine Shorny.

Did a bleak future await me? After all, I was born in a welfare hospital to an alcoholic who had been unfaithful to her husband. This woman and her husband, also an alcoholic, would raise me. Was there any hope for me?

To the world there seemed to be no hope, but powers greater than this world held my life. With the help and grace of God and the strength given to me, along with the people in my life, not only would I survive these rough beginnings, but I would thrive into a life of abundance and wholeness.

Chapter 1
Death and Redemption

"Come get me. Come get me! I want out!" I screamed as I shook the crib railing with my small hands. Hearing Patrick and my mother laughing in the kitchen told me they were not coming to get me. I got even more frustrated, yelled louder, and shook the rail harder.

I was three years old, and if they were not going to help me, I could get out by myself. I did not need their help.

They laughed when I toddled into the kitchen. They had known all along that I could get out by myself as I had done many times before. That self-determined spirit would vault me over higher barriers in my life than that of a crib railing.

This happened at the first place I remember living. It was a small, dark house on 33rd Street in Lincoln, and the crib I slept in was in Frank and Josephine's bedroom.

Even though my beginning was meager and some may have felt there was little hope for me, the first three years of my life were not bad. I had a family—mother, stepfather, and older brother. Although they didn't provide for me as well as they should have, I didn't know the difference.

From the time I was ages three to ten, we moved frequently—eleven houses in seven years. No matter where we lived, there were always neighbor children around. This was true of the house on 33rd Street. I would run after Pat when he went outside to play with his friends. "Wait Patrick, wait for me. I want to come, too," I would yell as he ran ahead of me.

"Well, hurry up if you're coming. I don't have all day. The guys are waiting," Pat answered in a hurried voice. He did not slow his pace for me, so I ran as hard as I could to catch up with him. But when I got to his side and held his hand, he pulled me along rather than shaking me off.

Behind our house, there were many trees where the boys climbed or played hide-and-seek. I always stayed with Pat when he hid. At age three, I was too scared to go off with any of the other children. When they got tired of playing hide-and-seek, or if it was too hot to run, they found something else to play.

One of these games was Swinging in a Blanket. The smallest kids were the ones who got to swing. Since I was the smallest—not yet four—they enjoyed swinging me the most. The boys laid the blanket on the ground, and I lay down in the middle of it with my legs and arms straight. Then the biggest boys took the two corners at the end of the blanket and folded it up around me. Inside was dark and cozy. My body tingled because I knew what was coming. As they picked the blanket off the ground, I felt my body move. It started out slow and smooth; then they swung me higher and higher, faster and faster. It felt like I was flying back and forth through the air. The feeling of flying filled me with joy, and I laughed and screamed at the same time. The higher they went, the louder I screamed. Pure fun!

Some days my mother Josephine and I took the bus downtown and met her mother, Grandma Mahoney. Grandma shopped or paid bills. Then we went to the bus stop to ride the bus back to her house. When we got to the bus stop,

Grandma Mahoney, Kathy and Pat

Grandma motioned for me to sit by her. Her face looked soft and squishy, and I loved it when she gave me a warm smile. She would wrap her arms around me as I sat beside her on the bench. Then I pulled her other arm from her lap and looked at the watch on her wrist. I loved putting her watch up to my ear and listening to the smooth, rhythmic tick, tick, tick. Soon the bus came, and she gently nudged me to sit up.

The large bus with bright, colorful polka dots on the side, like a bag of Wonder Bread, pulled up in front of us. As the brakes gave their long screech, the smell of diesel filled the air. I loved that smell even though it was strong and a wave of nausea sometimes came over me. We stood up but never moved toward the bus until it stopped. I held onto Grandma's hand as the door slid open with a screech. Grandma let me go ahead of her, still holding my hand. The steps seemed huge, but I tried to keep my balance as I lifted my legs as high as they would go: one, two, three steps.

Inside the bus I smelled the diesel again, but not as strong as outside. I waited until I heard the coins clink down the tall, glass money box, and then we found a seat. Grandma let me sit by the window. I looked through the glass and held onto the leather seat ahead of me as best I could with my short arms. I tried to steady myself as the first jolt came from the bus edging forward. Then I settled back for the short ride to Grandma's house.

Little did I know that my relationship with Grandma Mahoney would be cut short. On October 7, 1963, two months after I turned four, she died. Uncle Buck (his real name was Frank, but my mother always called him Buck) and Grandma were driving home from David City when they had a one-car accident that killed them both. Grandma died instantly, and Uncle Buck, pinned in the car, died later.

The news report in the David City paper said:

> "We don't know exactly what happened," said Highway Patrolman Carl Grossoehme, "the driver apparently lost control of the car, crossed the road and hit a concrete culvert nosing the car into the ground and then it flipped or rolled over two or three times."
>
> That is the way the patrolman described the fatal accident that took the lives of a son and his mother early Sunday morning 1½ miles North of Ceresco.
>
> There were no witnesses to the accident, said Grossoehme.
>
> Killed were Mrs. Clara Mahoney, 73, a passenger in the car driven by her son, Francis, who died in the Saunders County Community Hospital about two hours after the one-car crash. Mrs. Mahoney was killed outright when she was thrown from the car.

> *Passer-bys drove to Ceresco and notified Lyle Gamble, policeman, who, in turn notified the authorities and called the Wahoo First Aid Squad. The driver, who was pinned in the wreckage by his left leg, was freed after about a half hour and rushed to the hospital, but his condition was critical. Both were from Lincoln. The car was a total wreck.*
>
> Used by permission from the *David City Banner Press*

When this happened, I was four, and we were still living in the house on 33rd Street. Dona came to our house early in the morning. I had been asleep in my crib but woke after hearing a knock on the front door and Josephine getting up. They sat in the living room, and Dona gave my mother the horrible news. Josephine ran back to her bed and threw herself down. From my crib, just beside the bed, I saw her body rolling back and forth as she screamed hysterically and cried.

Pat got out of bed and peeked into the room. Because of the screaming and loud voices, he was cautious and didn't come all the way in. Our parents often fought, especially when they were drunk, so he was careful when hearing loud angry voices coming from the bedroom. But this was not Frank and Josephine's usual fighting.

"If Buck wanted to kill himself, why did he take Mama with him?" Josephine said through her sobs. "If Buck didn't want to go back to jail, why did he kill Mama, too?"

"Come on, Jody, you know that's not true." Dona's words were calm at first, but as Josephine persisted with this thought, I could see Dona's face getting angrier and angrier. Then Dona cursed at Josephine, and I thought she might hit her. Pat must have seen the fear in my eyes because he lifted me out of my crib. We went into the kitchen.

Soon Dona came in and told Pat and me to sit with her on the couch. When she told us what happened, Pat started crying, but I didn't understand. To a four-year-old, death means nothing. I just knew my mommy was sad and angry, and whenever she felt sad and angry, I did too.

As time passed, I missed my grandma. I didn't remember my Uncle Buck. The only time I had seen him was when our family visited him in the Lincoln prison earlier that year.

That had been a new and unsettling experience for me. The prison was unlike anything I had ever seen. The building was huge and built of concrete and steel. The only other large buildings I'd seen had been a doctor's office and schools, and this one looked much different. We left our car in the parking lot and walked to the door. I held my hand over my eyes to shield them from the hot, late-August sun. Going into the building gave no relief from the heat. Outside it was hot, but at least the wind was blowing a little.

Inside the air stood still and the smell was not good. I recognized the cigarette smell, but there were other disgusting smells that made me want to hold my nose, but Pat had once told me that was not a nice thing to do. Instead, I used my fingers to plug my ears. Just like the outside of the building, the inside was all metal and concrete, so the clanging as a door shut amplified off the hard walls.

I didn't know why we were there, and the noises and smells bothered me. I didn't like it there so as my mom talked to a man inside a window with bars across it, I went to Pat.

"Carry me," I begged.

"You're four years old now; you're too big to be carried," Pat said. Because I had just turned four only a week before, he and my mom were trying to get me to do more on my own. But I was scared and wanted protection. I went to Frank and held up my arms. He picked me up and held me so my head could rest on his shoulder. I felt safe being held by Frank in this place. In the prison with Mom, Pat and a lot of other people around, we weren't alone in a dark room and Frank wasn't drunk. He wouldn't hurt me here and I believed he really did care about me. It's strange how I felt so close to Frank in this situation and afraid of him at other times. But that's how it was with Frank and me. I don't remember any specific abuse from him, although it may have happened when I was very young. But, I never felt safe and comfortable with him. I was afraid to be alone with him. And I was afraid of him when he was drunk. Much later a family member told me Grandma Mahoney had witnessed him mistreating me when I was one or two.

So in the prison I felt safe. I closed my eyes and rested my head on his shoulder. As Frank walked, I opened my eyes to see where we were going. We went down a long hallway and into a huge room. It had tables and chairs in the middle and benches along the wall that looked like restaurant booths, only with no table in between. Our family sat down in one of the booths.

Soon a man dressed in a green shirt and pants came out and sat with us. Josephine gave him a big smile and hug. Frank said, "Hi," and Pat and I were silent. This must be Uncle Buck, I thought. The adults talked for a while, and then he looked at me and tried to get me to say something. However, I was a shy child around strangers, and even though he was my uncle, he was still a stranger. He asked me if I liked gum and pulled out a stick of Doublemint, my favorite. My eyes lit up in a big smile as I took the gum. I'm sure this pleased him. Why he paid any attention to me at all I couldn't understand, but his offer of a stick of gum made me realize he wanted some kind of connection with me.

As a small child, I did not know my Uncle Buck had been a paratrooper in World War II. But his bravery as a soldier did not help him with the addictions he faced back home. He was

Uncle Buck

in prison for writing bad checks. However, as a young child, I neither idolized nor judged him. I just remembered him as a nice man who gave me gum. The accident took Uncle Buck out of my life forever, and I would never have the chance to know him.

After the accident I missed my grandma and realized she also was gone from my life forever. However, I dealt with most of my sadness by myself. Sometimes I went crying to Pat. When he asked me what was wrong, I told him I missed Grandma. He tried to comfort me, but I'm sure he too was mourning the loss. Showing his own emotions and giving comfort to his little sister did not come easily to an eleven-year-old boy. I was thankful for the little comfort he gave me. He was the only one I could turn to.

My mother's grief was so huge that it also became my grief. Most of her emotions became mine. I tried to comfort her and keep her calm so I would be safe. If I didn't, her emotions erupted, and she turned violent. This was the price I paid for my mother's alcoholism. An addiction to the bottle consumed her, and little of her was left to care for me.

The impact Grandma's death had on my mother was worse than anything I had seen her go through. This death was tragic because Grandma and Grandpa Mahoney were the only people Josephine felt loved her. Even though she was the oldest of four sisters and one brother, she was also the one who needed the most help from her parents. William and Clara Mahoney, children of immigrants from Ireland and Czechoslovakia, were kindhearted and generous. They knew their oldest daughter was not a strong person, but they did not believe she was using them. She just needed help, and they always gave it to her.

As a child, Josephine had been bright until the day she fell out of a tree; after that she did not do well in school. In the 1920s and 1930s, no formal diagnoses of her physical or mental health were made, but she definitely had been affected. Because of this, her parents offered her extra help and support.

When she needed money, they gave it to her. When she needed food, they gave it to her. If she needed a place to live, they helped her set up a household. However, they never held her accountable for her poor choices — her alcoholism, spending habits, or choices in men. Trying to do their best, William and Clara acted out of love for their daughter, and this love may have made her weak and needy as she was always relying on others, especially her parents, for help. Her father, a farmer and railroad worker, had died in 1960, due to a blood clot and heart problems. Now both of Josephine's parents were gone.

The deaths of Grandma and Uncle Buck had an even more profound impact on Josephine because she felt partially to blame. The day Grandma Mahoney and Uncle Buck were killed and Dona came to tell us about the accident, Josephine's response was, "If Buck wanted to kill himself, why did he take Mama with him? If Buck wanted to die so he wouldn't have to go back to jail, why didn't he leave Mama at home?" Josephine believed Uncle Buck was trying to commit suicide through this accident. Her comment made Dona mad that day, so mad that she almost hit Josephine. If Pat and I had not been there, she probably would have hit Josephine just to shut her up.

Dona was Buck's ex-wife, and she believed he would never try to take his own life. As a child, however, I always believed Uncle Buck had tried to kill himself in that accident. This belief about the accident was Josephine's way, either consciously or unconsciously, to make up for the guilt she felt in believing she had played a part in it.

Grandma and Grandpa Mahoney

This is the version of the story later told to me: A week before the accident Josephine and Frank had been in David City with Uncle Buck and Grandma Mahoney. Josephine was drunk and got angry with one or both of them. She refused to give them a ride back to Lincoln, leaving them stranded in David City. They had to borrow money from someone to get a ride home. The next Saturday night Grandma and Uncle Buck went back to David City to repay the money. On their return to Lincoln, they died in the accident.

Josephine's guilt over this incident must have scarred her deeply. She became depressed. All day she sat on the couch and stared ahead. The curtains were always drawn, so the house was dark. The only light came from the TV and the little that came through the spaces on the sides of the windows the curtains didn't cover.

As in many families of poverty and abuse, one horrible event may cause a spiral of other difficult things. This was true of our family as well. One of these times was my stepfather Frank getting shot or beaten up. I don't know exactly what happened, but I remember a great deal of anxiety in the house one night and people yelling in the alley or at the back door of our house. Frank rushed in the back door, and Josephine helped him into the shower. Josephine told me to stay out, but I peeked around the corner. From what little I could see, Frank was bruised and bloody. He was also upset and anxious. The tension in the house was high, and I was scared.

After this, Frank was out of our lives for a while. I don't know if he was wanted by the law or mad at Josephine, but he was gone. This made Josephine's depression worse.

Because of her deepening depression, Josephine lost nearly all her ability to parent Pat and me. This became a near-fatal situation for Pat when he developed appendicitis. The pain started as just a small ache in his stomach, so he stayed home from school. Instead of easing, the pain got worse. He didn't go to school for several days and lay in bed. The pain became greater with each passing day.

Our mother let him stay in bed for several days, moaning

in pain. This did not mean she was cruel or didn't care. Her depression and alcoholism consumed most of her life, and this did not leave much room for anything else, even the love she had for her children. During this period in her life, she had no husband, no phone, no car, and no driver's license. Due to these circumstances, she probably felt helpless to do anything for Pat. His pain eventually became so severe she could no longer ignore it and finally got help. She probably walked to a pay phone or used a neighbor's to call Aunt Dona. Pat made it to the hospital and had the surgery before his appendix burst.

Depression can be a fatal illness. I don't know how close Josephine was to taking her own life, or if she would have been able to pull herself out of this depression. But two uninvited guests came to our house. They helped her start the healing process and may have saved her life. I believe God sent them.

Chapter 2
Opening Presents Before Christmas

It was late October or early November of 1963 and I was still four years old when strangers came to our door. I sat at the kitchen table, my crayons spread out and a coloring book in front of me. I heard the first knock, but I wanted to finish coloring the blue petals on a flower, so I didn't look up. When I heard the second knock, I looked over at Josephine. She was sitting on the couch, smoking a cigarette, and staring at the TV.

"Mommy, someone is knocking at the door."

She looked at me. "Who is it?"

"I don't know."

"Well, go answer it."

I walked to the door and turned the knob. It wouldn't open and I realized the big lock on the top was turned. "I can't. It's locked."

Josephine sighed as she got off the couch and came to the door. I was hoping it would be Aunt Dona. She came sometimes during the day to take us to the grocery store and other places.

As the door opened, I saw two strangers standing there, a man and a woman. They were dressed in nice clothes. The woman wore a pretty, dark blue dress, and the man had on black pants, white shirt, and black necktie. I stepped behind Josephine, hiding between her legs. These people didn't seem mean, but they were strangers, and that made them scary.

Josephine talked to them a little. They told her their names and pulled out a little newspaper from the big square, black purse they were carrying. This newspaper was smaller than a normal newspaper, more like comic book. It also had pictures on the front. If they had brought comic books to look at, this could be interesting, I thought. But as I peeked around and got a better look, I saw the pictures were not from comic books but of a big building and people who didn't look happy. No, this was not interesting, I thought and hid behind my mom again.

Then my mother and the two people sat on the couch and talked.

"Kathy, why don't you keep coloring," my mom told me. So I went back to my coloring book, but I could see and hear them from the kitchen. Soon I heard my mom talking about Grandma Mahoney and how she and Uncle Buck died in the car accident. She started crying as she told them how much she missed her mom and how sad and lonely she was. Then the strangers talked about stuff I didn't understand, so I went back to my coloring.

As a young child, I did not know anything about grief therapy, but this meeting with the strangers was a kind of therapy for my depressed mom. She poured out all her sorrows. They listened and gave her hope.

I will always be thankful to these people for coming to our house that day. I will always be grateful to Jehovah's Witnesses who take their faith seriously and go door-to-door talking to people about God. To some people, who have a firm handle on their faith or don't really care about God, the Jehovah's Witness approach can seem pushy. But for Josephine, who felt hopeless in the depths of depression, this was just what she needed. They witnessed to her, invited us to church, and brought us hope. This helped us out of the despair and depression that had engulfed Josephine's life.

Soon our family started attending the Jehovah's Witness Church on Holdrege, just off 27th Street. It was a wonderful place to be. The people were nice, and no one there was drinking, getting drunk, or angry. In this environment, I started to open up and be myself without worrying about the adults. They helped my mom by giving her friendship and positive support. Because of this, she was able to take better care of Pat and me. This relieved some of my fear and replaced it with more security and hope.

The best part of this church was the pastor and his family. They took us under their wing. The pastor and his wife had a teenage son and daughter who were nice to me.

They took care of me when Josephine had to run errands or had to go to appointments. I remember being at their house, eating meals, playing games, and just hanging out. Compared to most of the houses I had lived in, theirs was a palace. This was not because it was big or expensive; in fact, it was a modest home. However, it was clean and smelled good. Also, no piles of junk cluttered the rooms, and it didn't smell like tobacco and alcohol.

Theirs was a calm and happy home, and I didn't worry that someone was going to erupt in anger at any moment. There was good food at meal times, and, whenever I was hungry, I could ask for a snack. It was a house of abundance, not a house of lack. In the homes I lived in with my family, there was always some kind of need: for food, for peace and calm, for clean spaces, for love and security. Being with this pastor's family was a welcomed relief for me. This family was so different from mine. What I didn't realize as a young child was that this was the norm and our family was so different from the way most people lived.

We were still attending the Jehovah's Witness Church, although not regularly, in the fall of 1965, when I turned six and entered school. I could have entered school when I was five, but I had a late summer birthday and developmentally I was not ready. My social development was the main issue. I was extremely shy and had difficulty talking to anyone unfamiliar. I think Josephine saw I was not ready for school because she had help from the church. She talked to the principal, and together they decided I should wait another year.

Kindergarten was a new adventure in my life, and I enjoyed it. School was a clean, happy place, and I felt safe there. They gave me food, a morning snack. The adults weren't drunk. Plus, if I did what they asked me to do, they were usually nice to me. The school's consistency and guidelines helped me know what to expect. This was a welcome relief for my developing brain, which up to this point had lived with a lot of stress and chaos caused by the poverty and alcoholism in our family. Also, the other children didn't realize how poor I was. It probably didn't matter to them.

Family life was getting to be more normal. Frank had come back. That Thanksgiving he and Josephine cooked a turkey all night in the oven. I thought that was so cool. On Thanksgiving morning, we woke to the wonderful smells of food cooking.

Christmas that year was also great. As followers of the Jehovah's Witness church, we didn't celebrate the birth of Jesus in a commercial way with gifts and a Christmas tree. But luckily for Pat and me, Josephine had not told the social service agency that we were not celebrating Christmas that year. Even though our family was doing better, it didn't mean we were able to go off welfare. We still received welfare checks, food stamps, clothing vouchers, and Christmas gifts.

In mid-December, a social worker knocked on the door with a couple of gifts for Pat and me. The social worker's gifts were not the only presents we got for Christmas, but they were usually the only store-bought, brand-new toys we got. Josephine often got us something, such as toys or clothing, but those came from the thrift store. Her gifts were something she liked and thought we would also like, but often we didn't. We weren't ungrateful, but just normal children who liked toys.

That year, when the social worker brought the presents, Josephine and I were the only ones at home. We were polite and thanked her, but as soon as she left, I turned to my mom.

"Can we open them now? Please, please?" I begged. "We're not celebrating Christmas this year so can we please open our presents?" Josephine had made a big deal about us not celebrating Christmas that year. Pat and I didn't like not having a Christmas tree, but if it meant we got to open our gifts early, it was worth it.

Josephine thought for a while as I stood in front of her, my hands pressed together in a prayer posture, my face squeezed tight as I continued to mouth, "Please, please, please?"

Finally she said, "When Pat and Daddy come home, we'll open the gifts." My little body sprang up with excitement.

The couple of hours until Pat and Frank got home seemed like an eternity. I tried to distract myself with cartoons and my Barbie dolls, but everything I did made me think about the gifts sitting on the table. When Frank and Pat finally got home, I ran to Pat and told him the great news.

"We get to open our presents right now."

Josephine stepped in. "No, let's wait until after supper, then we can all sit around and open them."

Pat and I quickly began our protest. We chimed in, speaking at the same time. "No, no, no. We want to open them now. You said so. It's not fair." Josephine tried to stand her ground with us until Frank stepped in.

"Oh, hell, Jody, let the kids open them," he said. "Who gives a shit if you're not going to wait until Christmas?"

That settled it. Josephine looked at us and said, "Okay."

I ripped into my gift. This felt like a victory for all kids everywhere to be opening gifts before Christmas. It was a victory for Pat and me. Being children of alcoholics, our lives, like the lives of our parents, focused on addiction. There wasn't much room left for the needs of the children. Opening the Christmas presents early was something we wanted, and neither our parents nor their addictions took it away from us.

My present was a Barbie house. I loved Barbie dolls, and this gift, a square, plastic Barbie house that opened up into four rooms and then folded down flat, was perfect for me. The fact that I got to unwrap it before Christmas was like breaking the rules and that made it extra special.

That was the last good thing I remember happening in our life because of the Jehovah's Witness church. Our relationship with them started to go downhill when Frank came back into the family. He didn't like the church or the people.

He didn't like the hold they had on Josephine; he wanted to control her.

Chapter 3
Ulysses

Soon after Christmas, Frank wanted us to move. He had a job in Ulysses, a small town an hour northwest of Lincoln. He was going to work for a farmer there. It was great that he had a job. I don't remember him having consistent employment otherwise. He often would go to employment agencies and get temporary jobs, but they never seemed to last long.

Another reason Frank had for moving was to get us away from Lincoln and the Jehovah's Witness church. That winter, in the middle of my kindergarten year, we moved from the school that I loved and the only town I had ever lived in. Even though there were many things we were losing, we were excited about Frank's job and about being together as a family. Maybe we could make a fresh start in a new town. So we left behind everything we had known, hoping we were moving toward a new beginning.

Ulysses was not a bad town. It was much smaller than Lincoln. Everyone knew everyone else, so we were definitely outsiders. No matter where you are, there are always some outcasts and misfits in need of friends, and those kids were ones Pat and I played with.

The house we moved into was one story with a couple of bedrooms and a large front porch. Due to lack of maintenance and proper upkeep, it was old and run-down. I'm sure the rent was cheap; that would be the only way we could have lived there. Like all our houses, it had a lot of junk and clutter. Because of her alcoholism and depression, Josephine was not a very good housekeeper. Our house had lots of things left lying around and boxes that were never unpacked.

Despite Josephine's many failings as a mother, she did show us a loving side of herself when she was not influenced by alcohol. I remember coming home on Valentine's Day that year with a special art project I had made in my kindergarten class. It was a heart with a face and paper accordion-folded arms and legs. I worked hard on cutting the heart and folding the paper and was proud of what I had done. I wanted to give my mom a nice gift, but more importantly I wanted her to be proud of me.

Because kindergarten let out at noon, Pat was not with me as I walked home. That winter day was cold and windy. The wind blew hard, and I was cold as I tried to hold onto my little Valentine man. I didn't put it in a bag because I wanted it to stay nice and not get smashed or broken. The whipping wind pulled my Valentine man back and forth. I held onto it tightly, but the glue that attached his small accordion legs could not withstand the wind, and they blew away. I burst into tears. The tears, mixed with the cold, blowing wind, made my face hurt and sting. I ran home. Josephine must have seen me coming because she came out to meet me. She asked me what was wrong. I held up the little Valentine man and through my sobs I told her the whole sad story and that I wanted to give her something nice for Valentine's Day. When I finished, she pulled me close and gave me a big hug.

"This is a perfect Valentine man, and I love it just the way it is," she said. She lifted me into her arms and carried me home.

I had wanted to bring something good into my mother's life. I'd thought if I did everything right and made her happy, then I could save our family. When my attempt to bring a little goodness into our life failed, I was devastated. Fortunately, Josephine was able to care for me that day.

Sadly, it wasn't long until things started to go downhill for us. Frank lost his job at the farm. Then one night, close to bedtime, the police came to our house and took Frank away.

I was in the bedroom with my mother and Frank. I was probably saying good night to them although I may have slept in the bedroom with them. I don't remember having a room of my own in this house. I heard a loud bang on the door. From the window, I saw flashing lights from the top of the patrol car.

Then I heard a booming voice. "Frank Shorny, open up. It's the police."

Panic filled the room. "Frank, what do they want?" Josephine asked as she sat in bed.

"Oh, who the f—— knows? They're probably trying to pin something on me. I didn't do anything."

I saw disbelief on Josephine's face, but she knew better than to challenge or question him, especially when he was this angry. She wanted to believe him, just as I did, but the truth was he had done something to bring the police. Maybe he had stolen something from the farm where he worked or had been playing cards at a bar and written a bad check. It didn't really matter what he had done. What mattered was that his arrest meant our family was being sucked down the toilet again.

Another bang came from the door. "Open up," boomed the voice.

Pat was there and opened the door. The next thing I remember is a police officer in the bedroom and another standing in the living room. The one in the bedroom was saying something to Frank as the officer turned him around, put his hands behind his back, and handcuffed him. They led him out of the house and put him in the car. The three of us stood on the porch and watched as the police car pulled away and its lights flashed until we could no longer see them.

This experience with the police shaped my view of them in a powerful way. I did not feel that the police were my friends or protectors. It felt like our whole family was on the wrong side of the law that night.

Over the next couple of days the mood in our house was heavy and sad. The bottom had fallen out again, and we didn't know what would happen. We stayed in Ulysses in the same house until Frank got out of jail. It was scary not having Frank around, but it was also relaxing. His support held our family together and without him we didn't know what would happen. But when he was there, he and Josephine were drinking and fighting.

After Frank got out of jail, we stayed in Ulysses for another month and then moved back to Lincoln. It was a warm day at the end of May when we packed up whatever fit in our car and left the rest for the landlord to deal with. I had been invited to the birthday party of one of my classmates and was really looking forward to going. I had bought a little coloring book and a small box of crayons to give her as a gift. But because we were leaving, I didn't get to go to the party. My family's circumstances robbed me of this afternoon of fun. This was the first of many celebrations and parties I would either never be invited to or be unable to attend.

We dropped the gift off on our way back to Lincoln. But as we drove out of town, we knew we had no money and no place to stay. We didn't know where our next meal was coming from or where we would sleep that night.

Chapter 4
The Condemned House

As we drove to Lincoln, Frank and Josephine talked about what we would do, where we would go. They decided to try a few friends and Aunt Dona first.

We went from place to place, but no one would let us stay with them. The people who refused us lodging that night were not cruel or unkind. Our family was always in need of something and never afraid or embarrassed to ask for a handout. Our attitude was that if others had something, they should share with our family. Working to have nice things wasn't important; it was the responsibility of others to take care of us. Frank and Josephine were truly a bottomless pit. I think the only reason anyone helped them anymore was because of Pat and me.

We ended up at the City Rescue Mission. This was different from a homeless shelter because it was usually only for men. In 1966 there were no homeless shelters for families, at least none that were an option for us that night.

We ate supper at the mission, sitting at a long table with

strange men all around us. I felt scared around them. The whole time we were at the mission, I stayed close to my family, always holding someone's hand or sitting on someone's lap. We attended a worship service after supper. When it was time to go to bed, there was no family room for us. Instead, there was just one large room with many cots lined up in rows. That was where we slept.

I don't remember how many nights we stayed there. It could have been more than one night, but it was not many. When we left the mission, we still did not have a place to stay. Fortunately, Frank and Josephine found a house. The city had condemned it, but we moved in anyway.

The house was on Leighton, the last house on a dirt road. There was a grain elevator on the other side of the street. From the outside, it looked old and rundown; it was definitely the worst house on the block. It stood in stark contrast to the other houses even though the other houses were far from new.

The inside of the house was bare. There was at least one bedroom, maybe two, a living room, and a kitchen. It had no electricity or indoor plumbing, so we carried in all the water for cooking and bathing. In addition, the bathroom was outside: an outhouse. There was a wood stove, and Frank and Pat had to gather wood from wherever they could find it. We got water from a spigot outside.

Brown, sandy roofing material covered the outside of the house. Once I used the roughness of the house as a weapon. A younger neighborhood boy made me mad, and I pinned him up against the house, rubbing his hands up and down on the scratchy surface until he cried. This was a mean thing to do, but I did it to gain some control in my life. Because this child was smaller than me, I could overpower him. This is what I had experienced from the adults in my life.

Using physical violence or angry words was the way the grownups in my life solved their problems. It didn't matter who or what the problem was. If someone made them mad, there was no talking or trying to work things out, there was only physical violence or angry words. The main task of my childhood was to keep myself safe from this anger and violence. I did this by keeping the adults happy or just staying out of their way. However, I could not always manage this as a young child. One sad thing happened at this house, with a dog.

I loved animals, especially dogs. While we were living on Leighton, a small, brown stray started hanging around. He was a shy, timid dog so I wasn't worried about him being aggressive with me. I enjoyed playing with him. He wagged his tail when he saw me and let me pet him. Mostly he was just a comforting, relaxing presence in my crazy, chaotic life.

Josephine and Frank never paid much attention to the dog. They probably didn't want to have another thing they were responsible for. I took care of the dog as best I could. But I could not protect the dog from Josephine's temper.

One day Josephine was furious about something. I had been playing with the dog, and he had done something to make her mad. Her wrath was directed at him, and even though I was thankful it was not directed at me, I was afraid of what she would do. Little did I know that I would be forced to be a part of her violence.

The dog and I were outside when I heard her yelling from inside the house. I tried to hide him; however, she found us in the yard. Yelling at the dog, she grabbed at him, but the dog was too fast for her and quickly ran away. He would run to another part of the yard, sit there, and look at her. She tried to catch him again, but he just ran from her. She did this a couple of times, her anger mounting with each attempt. I was scared and wanted to run away. I wanted to do what I always did to stay safe, maybe quietly slip behind the house and then walk down the alley. Usually I would stay away until she cooled off. This time was different; I couldn't leave my dog. I feared what she would do if she caught him.

Finally, she stopped chasing the dog. Oh good, she's given up. Maybe she'll leave the dog alone, and he will be safe, I thought. But I was wrong. Instead of turning back to the dog and yelling at him, she turned to me and started yelling.

"Katherine, go catch that dog."

I did not say no, but as I hesitated, she walked toward me. She was not a large woman, but that day the force of her anger made her seem huge. She stood looking at me, her face tight with anger. As she pointed her finger at the dog, she screamed, "I said go get that dog, damn it!"

My head throbbed and my stomach hurt. I looked at the dog. He looked right into my eyes. I was his friend. We had a connection, and he trusted me. He didn't think I would do what I was about to do. Tears welled up in my eyes, but I had to hold them back. If I started crying, it would not evoke my mother's sympathy, but only anger her more.

Then I did it. I called the dog over to me. He looked at me with sad, confused eyes. What did I want? What was I asking him to do? He didn't know, so he just stood there as I slowly walked toward him. When I got close enough, I grabbed his collar and held him. Josephine walked over. By this time, she had found a weapon, a small stick from the yard.

When she got to us, she hit the dog with the stick, releasing the full volume of her anger with each blow. My stomach, chest, and shoulders shook as I struggled to hold back the tears, but I could not contain my sadness as tears welled up in my eyes. The dog yelped and whimpered as he struggled hard to get away. In an attempt to save his own life, he turned on me as he twisted his head and tried to bite my hand. Fear surged through my body and I quickly released my hold on the collar. He ran out of the yard and out of my life.

"Why did you let him go?" Josephine yelled.

"He was trying to bite my hand."

I guess Josephine got the release that she needed from hitting the dog because she didn't turn the stick on me. She threw it down and walked into the house.

I stayed outside and called the dog. He did not come. I knew he wouldn't come back. He had been a good friend, and now he was gone. Worst of all, I was the reason he left. Because of my fear, I had sided with Josephine and allowed her to beat the dog.

I went to the side of the house, sat down, and cried. Whether or not Josephine heard my sobs, she did not come to comfort me. I sat there alone. I had lost the one being in my life that gave me comfort. I cried for myself, and I cried for the dog. What would become of him? Would he find another place to stay and people to love him? Would anyone care for him, give him water and food? He was just a mangy old mutt. He was dirty and probably had fleas. No one seemed to want him or care for him.

That dog was a lot like me.

We lived in that condemned house for the summer and the first month of school. I started first grade at Washington Elementary School. This experience of school was much different from the first school I went to in kindergarten. I did not feel accepted by the other children or the teacher. For the first time, I realized how bad it was to be poor. Living in a condemned house with no electricity or water added to my look of poverty. The children we played with in the neighborhood probably told others at school where we lived.

I felt different from the other children, and I felt the teachers treated me differently. This became clear when our first-grade class performed a skit. I really wanted the role of the princess. I memorized the lines and was sure I would get it. The teacher said the girl who played this part would need to be in charge of the princess gown. It was a beautiful dress, and I was looking forward to wearing it.

When the teacher announced who would play the part of the princess, I was surprised. She gave it to some other girl who didn't have the part memorized. During the performance, she had to read the lines. It felt so unfair, and I couldn't understand why the teacher had given the part to the other girl.

Now I realize that if she would have sent the dress home with me it would not have been cared for. The teacher saw the shabby, dirty clothes I wore to school. She may have thought the dress would never come back. Also, if she chose me as the lead, my parents would probably not get me back to school for the performance. This is one example of subtle ways I was judged during childhood for being poor. I felt like people always saw the poverty; they never saw me or my abilities.

In the fall of 1967, we moved to a nicer house on Y Street, close to 27th Street. It was nothing fancy, but coming from the condemned house on Leighton, we felt like it was a mansion.

It was raining the night we moved in. Pat, Josephine and Frank were moving furniture, so I stayed out of the way. I found a bag of cookies and lay down on the couch. As the cookies filled my stomach with the joy of sugar, my mind filled with hope. Here we were in a new house, one that was a hundred times better than where we had lived before. I felt the hope and anticipation that I often felt when we moved into a new place. A new house is like a blank slate. It's empty and clean and you can put things where you want them and make everything look beautiful. And there's hope for all the new memories that can be made.

As I sat on the couch that night, listening to the rain and eating cookies, I had new hope for our family. Maybe our family would function normally in this house. Maybe this house would be a place where the parents didn't drink and fight, where there was always food in the cupboard, not just when we had food stamps, where the dad had a consistent job and the mom took care of the house and made good meals. Maybe in this house we would have company over. We would have birthday parties and Christmas celebrations. Maybe we would actually invite others over and not always go to someone else's house, uninvited at meal times, hoping they would feed us. I truly wanted a normal life, and I hoped it would start with this new beginning.

Chapter 5
Sacred Heart

In the fall of 1967, I entered second grade. I was in another new school and a different house. The house sat on the corner of 27th and R. Even though school was a good place for me, being in a different school, sometimes two schools each year until the sixth grade, added to the stress and chaos of my life.

School is supposed to be about education, learning, and making friends. It's also about figuring out the world and how you fit into it. But for me, a large part of my time at school, when I wasn't worrying about what had happened or would happen at home, was figuring out a new set of rules.

These rules weren't just the regular stuff, like where to go and what to do, but the unspoken information a child needed to know: who was safe and what did I have to do to please people. What did my teacher expect me to do even if she never told me she wanted me to do it? Were the lunch ladies nice? If I smiled at them, would they smile back? Was the janitor a safe person? Should I be afraid to be alone with him? This is knowledge many other children learned once and could continue to use year after year. But because I was in a different school every year, I had to figure it out over and over again.

Finding new friends every year was stressful too. I gravitated to the kids who didn't have friends. This was usually the only group that accepted me at any school. Because of this, I quickly formed my own identity as being different. Even today, it is sometimes difficult for me to accept my place or position in the groups I belong to. I often wonder do I really belong? Am I really accepted, or am I still a loser and an outcast just trying to fit in?

In second grade, I went to Sacred Heart School. This was a Catholic school in a poorer area of Lincoln. This was a good school, and I'm thankful Josephine made the effort to enroll me there. She wasn't raised Catholic, but that was the church she gravitated toward. Perhaps that was Frank's influence. I'm also thankful this private school accepted all children, whether or not we could pay.

From our house the school was close enough for me to walk. I walked to and from school and sometimes home for lunch. One day, when I went home for lunch, Frank was the only one there. Being alone with him did not feel safe to me, so I stayed out of his way. Asking him to get me something for lunch was out of the question, and he did not volunteer anything. It was probably the end of the month, which meant the welfare check and the food stamps had run out so the cupboards were bare. I found some popcorn and ate that. This helped reduce my hunger but certainly did not fill me up.

Back at school, my teacher, a nun, asked me what I had for lunch. Knowing she would disapprove if I told her the truth, I made up a big, long tale about what I wished I had eaten for lunch. She listened politely, but I'm sure she realized it was not true. I hoped she would not know I was lying. I knew it was wrong to lie, and I thought lying to a nun was worse than other kinds of lies.

Worrying about the sins I was committing was not as much of a priority as keeping myself safe from the sins that were happening to me. Pat was fifteen, and I was eight. He sexually abused me more often in this house. This abuse started when I was five and he was twelve. It usually happened when our parents were not around or paying attention. We must have shared a bedroom because I don't remember having a room of my own. Josephine and Frank may not have realized that having an eight-year-old girl and her fifteen-year-old brother share a room was inappropriate. Also, renting a three-bedroom house was too pricy for my family, so we had to make it work with only two.

The sexual abuse from Pat was constant grabbing and touching. He was always asking to see my body or have me look at his. I also had to deal with lewd inappropriate comments from him on a daily basis. His view of sexual prey had no boundaries, not even with his little sister. I was a girl, and in his worldview girls were meant for sexual gratification. The constant mauling, commands, and looks always kept me on guard. I feared they would lead to more violent actions.

Relationships in my family were complicated. Pat was an abuser, but he was also my brother. He was not a safe person for me to be with, but I felt safer with him than with Frank or Josephine. Even though I had to be on my guard with him most of the time, we were close and cared about each other. We were all each other had in this crazy, poor, unpredictable, alcoholic family.

One Sunday morning in early spring, I felt cared for by Pat. Our parents were gone, and somewhere we had found thirty cents. In 1968, this amount of money could buy a lot. Pat and I talked about what to do with the treasure we had found. We finally decided to buy pop at the corner gas station. Thirty cents was just enough for two bottles of Coca-Cola. Pat decided that I should be the one to get it. I guess it wasn't crazy to think an eight-year-old could walk one block, cross a busy city street, buy the pop, and carry it home. I agreed to do it, but I wished Pat would come with me.

I got to the gas station safely, bought the two bottles of icy, cold pop, and started to walk home. Half a block from our house the bottles started making my hands very cold. Then suddenly one of them slipped and crashed to the ground. It landed on the hard sidewalk and shattered into several pieces as the sweet, precious liquid escaped onto the street.

I started to cry. I was sad the pop was gone, but I was also afraid Pat might get mad at me and take the remaining bottle for himself. I held on tightly to the second bottle of pop and tried to stop crying as I walked the rest of the way home.

I got to the house and went inside. Bracing myself for Pat's anger, I held the bottle close to my body. Pat was sitting in the living room watching TV. He looked up. My tears had been contained to a whimper, but he could tell there was something wrong.

"What's the matter, Kathy?"

I held up the one remaining bottle of pop and starting crying again.

When Pat saw the single bottle, he came over to me. My body tensed. He kneeled down, looked into my eyes and said gently, "What happened?"

Through my tears, I poured out the story. When I was finished, Pat gave me a hug and said, "That's okay. I didn't really want pop this morning anyway."

This was a lie, and he was only saying it because he knew how much I loved pop. I tried to protest, but he insisted. So I went into the kitchen opened the bottle and poured it into two cups. Taking them into the living room, I settled in beside Pat. There we sat on a Sunday morning, watching TV, and sharing a bottle of Coke, just my brother and me.

Chapter 6
The Hunger in My Life

"Children, turn to page 25 in your spelling workbooks. Do activities A, B, and C. Work quietly and by yourself. If you have questions, raise your hand, and I'll come help you," Mrs. Smith said.

Mrs. Smith was my third grade teacher. We had moved to another house, this one on A Street. Park Elementary was the school for this year.

My body moved slowly as I opened the desk. I had stayed up too late, I thought to myself. Slowly opening my book, I tried to focus on the pages. I couldn't read the words. My eyes drooped, and my head felt funny. Then my body shook, jerking back and forth. My head hurt from the rapid movement. My arms and upper body were trembling, and I couldn't make them stop. I had never experienced this before. As fear filled my mind, I cried. It was terrifying for me to feel my body so out of control. Was I going to die? I wanted this to stop, but I had no control.

My body shook, and I cried deep, loud sobs. Soon my

teacher came over to me. She bent down and looked in my face.

"What's wrong with you?" she said in a voice more tender than I had expected.

I didn't know what was wrong. I was surprised by my own words. "I'mmm hungrrry," I said.

My teacher stood up and walked away from me. I sat there and continued to shake and sob. I knew all the other children were looking. No one was working activities A, B, or C in their spelling notebooks. Some were scared by what I was going through; others made unkind comments to each other.

"Why is she making such a fuss?"

"What's wrong with her?"

"Why doesn't she just eat at home like everyone else if she's so hungrrry," a boy sarcastically imitated me.

Then Mrs. Smith said in a sharp tone, "Quiet, children." I heard her push the intercom button and say, "Mrs. Higgins, could you come down here quickly, please?" For the first time I heard fear in her voice.

She came to my side, bent down, and put her hand on my shoulder. "It will be okay. Mrs. Higgins is coming to help you."

Mrs. Higgins was the school secretary. I was glad she was coming because she had always been nice to me. And even though she only saw the poverty and not who I really was, she pitied me instead of treating me like I was a dirty nuisance. Also, I knew Mrs. Higgins would get me out of this room and away from the other children.

Soon she was by my side. Kneeling down, she too asked me what was wrong. This time I had a little more composure and I whispered in her ear, "I'm really hungry."

She stood up and said in a matter of fact voice, like this was something she saw everyday, "Well, let's go to the office and see what we can do about that."

I tried to twist out of my desk, but I started to stumble as I stood up. Mrs. Higgins helped me up and put her arm around me. I closed my eyes and tried to bury my head in her side as we walked out of the room.

Back in the classroom, I heard Mrs. Smith say, "All right, children, the fun is over. Back to work, back to your spelling notebooks."

What fun? I thought as I walked down the hall. In the office, Mrs. Higgins sat me down in a chair right by her desk. She went into another room and came back with a carton of milk, a loaf of white bread, a jar of peanut butter, and a kitchen knife. She gave me the milk. I opened it immediately and began drinking. While I drank, she made me a sandwich.

After I finished the sandwich, I asked her if I could have another carton of milk.

"No, that's enough for now; lunch will be in an hour, and you don't want to spoil your appetite."

Spoil my appetite? I didn't think that was possible. I could drink five more cartons of milk and still eat three lunches. My stomach was usually hungry and rarely full, but for now my belly was partially full. This episode, whatever it was, had passed, and I was feeling normal again. Now it was time to go back to the classroom, and I didn't want to do that.

This experience affected me on several levels. I felt embarrassed because this had happened in class, in front of all the other kids. No one in the class had any sympathy for me, at least not that I can remember. When we went out for recess, some of the kids that I hung out with teased me and said I was faking it. Other children stared at me, talking behind my back about the stupid, poor kid.

This episode added to my belief that I was different, that normal people did not care about me and would never accept me, and that school was not a safe, caring place. Yes, they had given me food that morning, but that fed only my belly. What

I really needed fed was my spirit. I needed someone to see my situation, someone to care about me and not see only how my presence inconvenienced them.

The event also scared me. I had felt so out of control and thought I might die. This made a deep impression on my brain and sent a powerful message to my subconscious: "Food is life, and without food I will die." When a child is so hungry at school that she nearly passes out, it's hard to grow up and not see food as an extremely important part of life.

I'm sure the experience had a powerful influence on the teacher and secretary at school. I don't know if they called the child authorities or not. Mandated reporting of physical neglect was not required by school personnel in 1969. However, they probably called Aunt Dona, our emergency contact, because she brought us some food. Our whole life was an emergency, and members of the family, especially Dona, helped whenever they could.

For some reason, things became even worse at home in terms of money and food. One night I heard Josephine and Frank talking when I was in bed. They said if something didn't turn up soon, they'd have to start going through trash cans to find food.

Then another scary thing happened that may have been connected to our lack of food. Frank went missing for several days. We were all worried and didn't know what had happened to him. Josephine called people to try and find out where he was. But no one knew. We didn't know if he had left without telling us or was actually dead.

Finally, we found out he had been in jail for trying to steal a loaf of bread. When he came home, his story was that he had dropped the bread and was only trying to pick it up, not steal it. It's hard to know the truth. But to this day I believe that if someone is stealing food, they probably need it.

Food insecurity played a huge part in my childhood, but I

also dealt with emotional insecurity and lack of self-esteem. A lot of this came from not feeling accepted by most of the children at school. Fortunately, I had some friends in the neighborhood I felt safe with, and we enjoyed playing together.

I had fun playing with the neighborhood kids at their houses. One of the families had a camper trailer that we would pretend was our house. We fed our dolls smashed-up crackers mixed with water. The trailer was nice and cozy, just like a little house. In there, we could really have the kind of home and family we wanted. In our pretend world, families loved and cared for each other; they had food for their children and were free of alcohol and abuse.

The biggest part of my life was still my real family. In 1969, during the third grade, Frank was around more. This was good for the most part. I got to know him better that year. One good memory I have of him is when he bought a car. It was not new but newer than what we had had. He had been talking about this car, a green and white Rambler, and we were all excited about it.

I remember going to school one morning, hoping Frank would have the car when I got home so we could go for a ride. As I walked home that day, I saw Frank and Josephine in the new Rambler, driving the other way. They hadn't seen me, but I thought they must be coming to get me. I started running as fast as I could back toward school. As I ran, I hoped they wouldn't get to school, see that everyone had left, and drive back home. This thought made me run faster.

When I finally got back to school, they were just turning around to start back home. Thankfully, this time they saw me. They had just gotten the car and wanted to surprise me. We picked up Pat from his school and went for a drive.

Usually our drives took us to bars. Having anything new in our life was reason to celebrate, and celebrating meant going to a bar.

For Pat and me, being at a bar was fun for the first hour or so. Josephine and Frank were usually happy before they got too drunk. Pat and I enjoyed drinking pop until even we got our fill. Frank and Josephine bought us pop along with their beers. If we were hungry and wanted food, that was out of the question. Who needs food when you can have beer seemed to be their belief. They were happy with their beer, so we should be happy with our pop. But the fun quickly wore off for Pat and me as we grew hungrier and more tired.

Sometimes we were concerned because we had school the next day and needed to get our homework done. Staying home on a school night didn't seem to be a consideration for Frank and Josephine. On the contrary, the predominant attitude in the family was that adult needs outweighed child needs. Sometimes when it got very late and Pat and I were tired, they sent us to the car to sleep. However, we woke up when they finally came to the car, drunk and fighting with each other.

Alcohol was the main addiction, but my stepfather also gambled. He played cards, and then tried to pay off his losses with bad checks. I don't remember him playing cards at bars a lot. Maybe that was because one time things got ugly. As a child, I had no idea what really happened. What I do remember is that we were in a bar in another town, and people got angry at us. We had to get out quickly and go to our car. There were people yelling at us and coming after us. We got in the car and drove away.

Over the years I have often thought about this incident and wondered what happened. To a young child, a few people could have seemed like many. My guess is that Frank had lost at cards and couldn't pay for his losses; they knew his checks were no good so maybe some people in the bar wanted to beat him up or kick him out. Whatever happened, it was a scary experience and showed me that bars were not good places for children.

Besides their alcoholism, one reason Josephine and Frank may have wanted to go to bars was to stay away from the disgusting house we lived in. Our house on A Street was a real dump. The basement was especially bad. The entrance was on a small concrete slab outside the back of the house. When you opened the door, it smelled disgusting—like animals had been down there and used it for a bathroom. The only furniture was a single metal bed with a thin mattress. I went down there a few times, but it was nasty.

The part of the house I was in more often was my bedroom. This is the first house I remember having a bedroom of my own. It was a small, narrow room with a window at one end, a single bed, and a chest of drawers. Josephine never made an effort to clean up and never asked me to clean up either.

We found most of our stuff at dumps. Going to dumps was a favorite family activity. My stepfather picked up scrap metal and sold it at a junk yard to make extra money. This was fun for me as a child because there was always interesting stuff there: toys, dolls, books, old dishes. One time I found a beautiful blue satin, high-heeled shoe. I wanted to find the other one so I could play dress up at home. I didn't have anything so beautiful or fancy in my dress-up clothes. I looked and looked, sure the other shoe was there, but I never found it. All these things were someone else's dirty old trash, but to me they were treasures.

My family was happy at the dump. Usually my parents were not drunk or fighting. Because our parents were there, Pat wasn't molesting me. We were all together as a family, all of us happily doing our own thing, so I was free to be a child and let my imagination open up and run free. I imagined what I could do with the things I found or what I could make them into.

There were also many dangers there: broken glass to get cut with and nails to step on. One time we found a small bonfire that had burned out but was still hot. There was a nice metal pipe burning in it, and I knew Frank would like to have it. Wanting to please him, I reached down to get the pipe and burned my hand. It wasn't a bad burn. Josephine got out her hankie and soaked it in a puddle of water and wrapped my hand in it.

After our fun day at the dump or dumps (we often went to several), we would go to the junkyard. There we sold what Frank had found. We went to a junkyard on P Street and one under the viaduct on O Street. I remember the one on O Street best. We pulled the car in and weighed it on the large scale. Then we drove the car in and unloaded the metal. Then it was weighed again. Most of the time, Josephine and I went inside the office until this was done. Pat helped Frank empty the car.

Taking the scrap metal to the junkyard was another fun part of going to the dump. We got money for the metal and then we went to get something to eat or we'd go to a bar.

As an adult, I hear stories about families living in dumps in Third World countries. They survive off what they can find to sell and eat. Friends and other church members comment about what horrible living conditions these are, especially for children. As an adult, I also feel sad for children who have to live in dumps. And even though we never lived in an actual dump, I am also sad for myself that this activity, which my peers view as a horrible fate for children, was one of the best things about my childhood.

So my family went to bars and lived in dumpy, rundown houses, and those things were not fun. But going to dumps and getting new things, such as cars, was fun. The last car we got as a family was a '56 Ford Sunliner convertible.

When we got it, I didn't know it would be our last car. But something happened one day that told me things might be changing in our family. I was sitting on my bed, and a little bird came and sat on the windowsill. The bird pecked at the window. It kept pecking and pecking as if it were trying to get in. And I remembered that Josephine had said if a bird was at a window trying to get into the house, that meant someone was going to die.

Chapter 7
The Day Frank Died

"When we get back to town where should we stop? How about the Stardust?" Pat said as he sat in the front seat of the car. We were returning to Lincoln after going to many dumps that day in various small Nebraska towns.

I don't think Pat was talking to me. He was talking to our parents. But they didn't answer Pat, so I said, "No, let's go to a restaurant. I'm hungry. We could go to the one on Cornhusker. They serve pancakes all day. I'm hungry for pancakes."

Pat ignored my comment and leaned forward in his seat so he could see past Josephine, who was sitting in the middle, and looked directly at Frank.

"Where do you want to go, Daddy?"

"I don't know. Let's just wait and see when we get back to town."

Frank didn't seem interested in Pat's question. When I looked at him, I saw why. He was looking at a pile of junk in some trees just beyond a farmer's pasture.

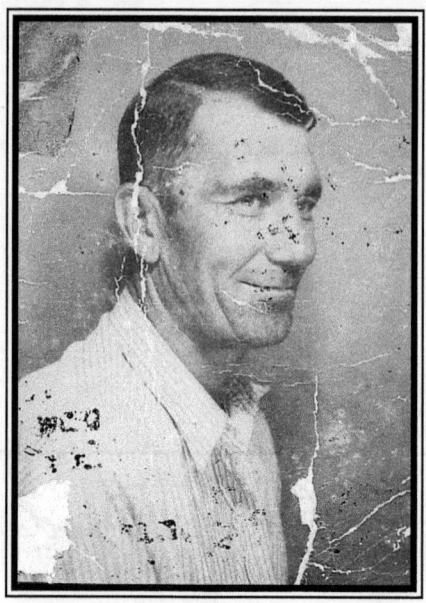

Frank Shorny

"Look over there, Patrick," Frank said and pointed to the pile. "It looks like there might be some good stuff in that pile."

We drove past the field and up to the house.

"Oh, Frank, can't we just skip this one and go home?" Josephine said.

Frank ignored her and got out of the car. "I'll just go and ask them if we can look through that stuff," he said.

Pat and I stayed in the car with Josephine. We both felt the tension rising from Frank ignoring Josephine. This tension was common for our family. The only question was whether the fight would start now or when Josephine got a few drinks in her. Alcohol lowered her inhibitions and increased her anger.

Soon, however, Frank was back in the car. He didn't say anything but backed the car out of the driveway and continued in reverse along the side of the road until he got back to the spot closest to the pile of junk.

"Come on, Patrick. Let's go."

Pat and Frank got out of the car and started for the junk pile.

I stayed in the back seat, which was overflowing with junk. The car smelled of the dirt and oil that clung to the metal and steel pipes, hubcaps and pieces of heating ducts, anything that would bring a couple of bucks at the junkyard. But the smell was not the only thing that bothered me. Sharp, jagged pieces of junk touched me, and I had to sit close to the car door so I wouldn't get cut. Sitting in the back seat with piles of junk was not a new experience for me. That day the junk collecting had been long and tiring, and I was anxious to get home.

It was the Monday after Easter, April 7, 1969. Neither Pat nor I had school that day. At breakfast, when Frank said we were going for a ride, I hoped it would be just for fun. I also hoped they would put the top down on the Sunliner. Our family had owned many cars, but never a convertible. When I first saw it, I was so excited. I imagined riding in it with my long, brown hair blowing in the wind. I would find an old pair of sunglasses and pretend to be a movie star. There were always convertibles in the movies. I loved going to movies and had decided I either wanted to be a movie star or a singer when I grew up.

We'd had the robin egg blue convertible for a month, but late March and early April in Nebraska was no time to put the top down, at least that's what Frank believed. However, today was the first day that felt like spring. The sun was shining, the winter snow was gone, and a warm breeze blew through the front car window and against my face. And so I had hope that maybe this would be a fun day. I hoped that we not only would put the top down on the convertible, but maybe we would visit someone, Aunt Dona in Havelock or Grandma Sekoris in Prague. And I really hoped we would not go from one bar to another, getting drunker with each stop, and end the day with a big fight. Oh, please, God, I thought, don't let the day end with them hitting each other or Josephine forcing me to walk home with her because she wasn't going to ride in the same car with that man. Please, God, not that. So many times when our family went out together, that was how the day ended.

Looking out the window, I saw Pat racing ahead of Frank. There was a cow out in the field, and Pat must have thought it was a bull. He started flashing the red lining of his jacket in hopes it would chase him. He had heard that bulls would chase anything red, like the matador's cape at a bullfight.

What a stupid idea, I thought. That cow isn't interested in the flashing red material. Anyway, who would want a cow to chase you? I was too afraid of large animals to get out of the car. I believed staying away from such a large animal was the smart thing to do rather than trying to get it to chase you.

As I was thinking about this, I heard the click of Josephine's cigarette lighter and smelled tobacco starting to burn. I was watching Frank and Pat make their way across the field when I saw Frank fall down. I thought he must have tripped over something and would soon get up. But he didn't.

When Josephine looked up from her cigarette, she too saw that he had fallen. She rolled down her window and yelled, "Patrick, Daddy's fallen. Go help him up." But when Pat got there and rolled him over we all knew something was very, very wrong. There seemed to be no life in his body. His body flopped like a rag doll. A wave of terror rolled over my body.

Josephine jumped out of the car and yelled to Pat, "Help him! Help him!" Pat must have known something about CPR because I saw him lean over Frank, breathe into his mouth, and press on his chest. With my face glued to the car window, my eyes filled with tears and my chest tightened. I could barely breathe as I watched this horror unfold. I heard Pat sob between breaths, begging, "Wake up, Daddy. Please wake up." But Frank just lay there, lifeless.

I was frozen in my spot by fear—fear of all that was happening, fear that if I got out of the car Josephine would force me to try to help Frank, and fear that the big bull was still in the field. I didn't want to take a chance on the bull attacking me, but I felt I should go help. Even though I was only in the third grade, I knew a little about CPR. Soon Josephine went out into the pasture, knelt down, and held Frank's body. This freed Pat to go to a nearby house and call for help.

Josephine just held him, she wasn't even trying to do CPR. I knew I should go help, but I was too afraid to leave the safety of the car, too afraid of the cow, too afraid of this new unknown. Finally, Pat came back and started CPR again. Soon I heard sirens and saw the ambulance racing down the highway.

The ambulance pulled up in front of the car. Several men pulled out a stretcher. They looked out over the field and saw where Josephine, Pat, and Frank were. They got to Frank, bent over, and examined him, checking his pulse and listening to his chest. Then they carefully lifted him up and put his limp body onto the stretcher.

As the people from the ambulance carried him from the field, I got out of the car for the first time. I ran over and held Josephine's hand.

"Do you want to ride with us or go in the car?" one of the men asked. He didn't seem to care what we decided; he just wanted to get the ambulance back to Lincoln.

Josephine looked at me and turned back to the man. "We'll ride with you." Then turning to Pat, she said, "Patrick, you drive the car."

So we climbed into the back of the ambulance. Two men worked on Frank all the way. I watched them as one pushed hard on his chest and another one breathed into his mouth. I kept hoping, praying they would stop and he would be okay. I wanted him to start breathing on his own, open his eyes, and look at me, but that did not happen.

At the hospital they wheeled him through some swinging doors and sent us to a waiting room. As we sat there, Pat rushed in. We were all in shock. We didn't say anything.

I looked around the room and saw a pop machine. A Coca-Cola would taste really good now, I thought. Knowing I couldn't ask my mom for money, I remembered my shoes. I was wearing penny loafers, and someone had given me two dimes to put in the tops instead of pennies. Two dimes, I thought, twenty cents, just enough to buy a can of Coca-Cola. But as I looked down at my shoes, I realized the dimes were not there. I had given them to Frank just before we got to the pasture. We needed gas to get home, and he didn't have enough money so I fished the dimes out of my shoes and asked if they would help. He said they would and he smiled at me and said, "Thank you, honey." I didn't know that would be the last time he would smile at me, the last time he would speak to me, the last time he would look at me. My eyes swelled with tears, and I started to cry. My mother put her arms around me, gave me a hug, and said it would be okay.

A man walked into the room and stood before us. He was dressed in a strange outfit, one I had never seen before. The pants and top looked exactly alike; they were gray and resembled pajamas. He wore a paper hat, and he pulled it off as he spoke.

"Hello, I'm Dr. Jones. Are you Mrs. Shorny?" he asked as he looked at my mom. She nodded and he continued, "I'm very sorry. We couldn't save him. His heart just wouldn't start again. From the paramedic's report, I imagine he was probably gone as soon as he fell down in the field. I doubt he suffered at all. Again, I'm sorry for your loss." As he walked away, Pat started crying, and Mom sat there with her arms around me.

Then something inside me broke. I started screaming, "No, no," and crying violently. A nurse walked up and asked if there was anything she could do to help. My mom said,

"No, she's just lost her dad." That was certainly true, but somewhere deep inside I knew I'd lost so much more. My family was not great, but they were my family. This was all I knew. It was where I belonged and where I felt somewhat safe. All that had changed now. Frank was gone. He wasn't a great father, but he was the anchor of this poor, dysfunctional family. Without him I had no idea how Josephine would act or what she would do. She couldn't drive, didn't work, and didn't know how to handle money. And when she drank, she was a mean drunk. Frank was the only one who could control her. Now he was gone and what little safety I had felt from him was gone too.

Chapter 8
Trauma and Aftermath of Death

Aunt Dona came and got us from the hospital, and we went to her house. The first person I saw when we got there was Steve, my safe cousin. He was the only male in my life who didn't try to take advantage of me. He was nice and treated me like a real person. I was never afraid to be alone with him because I trusted him and knew he would not hurt me. And on that horrible day I needed someone I could trust. As I walked through the doorway of the house, I felt numb. Even though I had been in this house many times, I felt confused and didn't know where to go.

"Come over here and sit down," Steve said as he took my elbow to guide me. "Let me get you some pop."

I sat in a chair and nodded. My chest felt heavy and tight as fear and sadness consumed me.

I couldn't speak and was too sad to cry. Frank was gone. I had seen him fall and watched the ambulance men work on his limp, lifeless body for twenty minutes on the way back to Lincoln. These images kept flashing in my head. Oh, why couldn't it have been different? Why didn't he wake up in the ambulance?

Soon Steve was by my side again, and he put a small, cool Dixie cup in my hand. I saw the wonderful brown liquid of the Coca-Cola. I heard the fizz, and as I brought it to my lips, I felt it dance on my face. The sweet liquid calmed my body as the sugar calmed the hunger in my stomach. The Dixie cup was an added bonus that Steve and I understood, but most of the adults did not. Dixie cups were a fun thing for us kids, but they were also special, and Aunt Dona rarely let us use them. More than once we were yelled at for trying to sneak one.

"Stay away from those bathroom cups. They're just for company. I don't want you kids using them all up," Aunt Dona's raspy voice would yell from another room.

So on this day, for Steve to bring my pop in a Dixie cup and Aunt Dona to allow it meant this was a special day—a sad special day. Steve's kindness comforted me, and I was thankful for that. Without words, he knew what I needed and did what he could to make me feel safe and comforted. That's the definition of a true friend.

As I drank the pop, the thoughts of the day once again filled my mind, and now tears filled my eyes. Steve moved close to me and gave me a hug. When I opened my eyes, Debbie, my other favorite cousin, was there holding a Barbie. Her happy, smiling face lifted my mood. I knew she didn't understand what had happened. How could she understand? She wasn't much older than I was when Grandma Mahoney died. She didn't understand the loss I felt, and like most of the people in the house that day, she was not sad that Frank died. No one in Josephine's family had cared about Frank in life, so why would they mourn him in death?

"Come on, let's go play." Debbie said as she held up the Barbie. The three of us headed into the bedroom she shared with her older sister, Gail. We went out of the adult world and into our child world of fantasy where we could control our lives and imagine we had all the things we longed for.

As the horrible day ended and the time for the funeral got closer, the numbness and confusion I felt were replaced with aches in my stomach and my head. These aches grew worse each day. I had always had stomachaches, due to the chronic stress and chaos in my life. Josephine often took me to the doctor, who gave me some white, chalky pills to take. I took a lot of those pills that week, but they didn't seem to help like they had before.

Two nights before the funeral, we were back in our house and Josephine was trying to help me go to sleep.

"Come on, sweetie, just try and relax," she said softly as her hand gently rubbed my stomach.

This was something she had done many times before when I had trouble sleeping. During this comforting time when I truly felt Josephine's love and care for me, I finally realized what had been bothering me for so long. I think I realized it on some level that first day at Dona's house when the adults talked about the funeral. This is how their discussion went:

"What's he going to wear?" someone asked.

"Does he have a suit or at least a nice shirt to be buried in?" another relative chimed in.

When Josephine came back from the funeral home after making the arrangements, she complained, "They won't even let me have the casket I want. He would love the dark wood with the beautiful green lining. Green was his favorite color."

Her voice cracked with emotion and then the anger came. "The only two they will let me choose from are just pine boxes with ugly linings."

She didn't realize or didn't want to realize that it would be a pauper's funeral. The state would pay for it because our family couldn't.

When Josephine mentioned the casket and all the adults talked about Frank's funeral, I got scared and uneasy. I knew, on some level, I did not want to see my Daddy in a casket. Because of all the sadness and stress, I had not realized this was the cause of my anxiety. But as I lay in my bed with Josephine trying to comfort me, trying to help me sleep, I was finally able to give words to my fears.

"I don't want to go to Daddy's funeral. Please don't make me," I pleaded as I looked into Josephine's face.

She seemed surprised, "What do you mean you don't want to go to the funeral? Of course, you have to go to the funeral; you're his daughter. The whole family has to be there."

"But I don't want to go. I don't want to see him all dead and lying in the casket. I want to remember him when he was alive."

Josephine looked at me with sadness and confusion. "Well, I don't know. I think you need to go to the funeral, but we'll talk about it in the morning. Go to sleep now. It's late." She stood up and walked out of the room.

When I woke up the next morning, my first thought was about Frank's funeral. As I walked into the kitchen, Josephine was sitting at the large round table, smoking a cigarette. Looking at her, I realized that the caring, comforting mother that had rubbed my stomach the night before was gone.

I sat across from her, not saying a word. Here was my sad, depressed, alcoholic mother. Even though she was not drunk, she still possessed that mean, uncaring attitude. Quietly I said, "I still don't want to go to Daddy's funeral. I don't want to see him in the casket."

"Well, you're going to his funeral. You're his daughter. People will think you didn't love him or care about him if you don't go. You're his daughter. You have to go." Her voice sounded angry and uncaring. After a pause, she continued,

"Dona's coming to get us in a little bit, so go get dressed."

I trudged back to my room. The pains in my stomach and head were back, and now I knew why.

Soon there was a knock on the door and I heard Dona come in, so I went to the living room.

As we put on our coats, Josephine said to Dona, "Kathy doesn't want to go to the funeral; can you believe that?"

I looked at Dona, expecting her to side with Josephine and have the same unyielding attitude about my skipping the funeral.

To my surprise she asked, "Why doesn't she want to go?"

Sensing my chance, I quickly jumped into the conversation, "I don't want to see Daddy in a casket. I want to remember him the way he was when he was alive, not laying all dead in a casket."

"That sounds reasonable, Jody. Why make her go?"

"Because if she's not there, what will everyone think? They'll think she didn't love her daddy. What will Frank's mom think? Kathy's his daughter. She should be at the funeral."

"For God's sake, Jody, don't worry about what Frank's mother thinks. Whether Kathy is at the funeral or not, it won't make her like you or accept your children any better. I can understand why she wouldn't want to see him in the casket. That stuff is scary for kids."

Josephine looked at me and back to Dona.

Even though Dona held a lot of power over Josephine, she wasn't yet convinced. "Come on, Jody, you need to do what's right for your kid, not worry about the relatives."

"Okay, I guess you don't have to go," Josephine said to me.

Relief flooded through me. I looked up at Dona. She smiled and gave me a hug as we walked out the door.

Dona's statement gave Josephine permission for me to miss the funeral. Dona was a tough cookie, but she was always there for our family. I never felt emotionally close to her, but

I knew she was a safe person and someone I could trust. Even though she might yell at me along with her children, I never worried she would hit me. She didn't get drunk and go crazy like Josephine, and I knew if she promised me something, she would follow through. Now, I was especially grateful to her.

On the day of the funeral, I stayed with Steve and Debbie at their house with Gail, my older cousin, as babysitter. When the funeral procession went from the church to the cemetery, Dona made sure they passed by her house. And when it came by, I was there, looking out the window. Seeing the hearse and knowing my daddy was in there was all the closure I needed. I don't think my nine-year-old traumatized mind could have handled anything more.

After the hearse had passed, Steve, Debbie, and I played and watched TV. Soon Dona and Josephine were back, and we all piled into Dona's 1967 Chevy station wagon and drove to my older cousin Sandy's house.

Most of the family from Josephine's side was there or at least the family members who felt okay with Josephine's lifestyle. There was a lot of alcohol and food at the party.

Frank had died just after Easter, so there were Easter cakes and cookies, some homemade and some bought from the after-holiday sales. Seeing all these goodies made me happy, but this was only one of many emotions I felt that day. I was sad. Frank was gone. He was the only father I had ever known. He was no ocean of fatherly love, protection, and comfort. But just like a person born in the desert has no idea there are springs with bounteous water in other parts of the world, I had no idea what a loving, caring, committed father was really like. I loved Frank and knew that on some level he loved me too. Now even this small trickle of fatherly love was gone forever, and I mourned that loss.

So how could I be happy that day and eat all of these delicious goodies? Eating sweet cakes and cookies made me happy. There were few positive things in my life, but food was one of them. Eating was a sensation my body enjoyed unlike other sensations that felt horrible. Also I worried that if I did seem to be enjoying myself, the other people might think I was a mean child and I didn't love my daddy. Josephine's worry about the funeral had become mine. I hadn't gone to the funeral and now I was enjoying all this food. What would people think?

But all the adults seemed to be having a good time, drinking and eating, and they didn't even notice me. I couldn't understand why they all seemed so happy, even Josephine. It didn't seem right that we were all having a party and enjoying ourselves because Frank was dead. No one asked how I was feeling, so I pondered these things on my own.

After the funeral things were supposed to get back to normal, but what was normal now? Who would we be without Frank? He defined each of us in good and bad ways.

Frank's death would certainly affect Pat and me. For better or worse, Josephine was now the head of our family. The way Frank's death changed her was what mattered most. Frank had controlled her, and I don't think she was ever free to say what she felt with him. So what would Josephine become without Frank's hand in her life? Would she gain strength and self-confidence? Or would she be even more controlled by her addictions and let herself fall into the risky behavior from which Frank had always tried to save her? Whatever direction her life took, Pat and I would be raised up or dragged through the mud along with her.

This was the summer of 1969, and many things were changing in our world. On TV I saw the first moon landing and heard about Woodstock, the Vietnam War, and the civil rights movement. Our family would be going through changes as well.

Chapter 9
The End Starts Here

On a Sunday afternoon a few weeks after Frank's death, Pat, Josephine, and I were sitting around the house, not knowing what to do. We couldn't go anywhere because Josephine couldn't drive. Even though Pat had driven our car to the hospital the day Frank died, Pat didn't have a license either. We felt sad and lonely.

"Let's look through Daddy's trunk," Josephine said.

"Yeah, let's do that. Maybe there will be some good stuff in there." When Pat said "good," what he really meant was something valuable we could sell. But when we opened the large trunk, I could tell Pat's thoughts turned from what he could get out of it for himself to his feelings for Frank.

The first things we found in the trunk were empty cans of tobacco and leftover cigarette papers. Frank never bought packaged cigarettes; instead he bought loose tobacco and papers and rolled them himself. I guess this was a cheaper way to smoke. We found some clothes, a few small pieces of metal, and a jar of pennies. Josephine took that. Mostly it was junk.

But it helped us connect with Frank and feel the pain of his loss all over again.

The last thing Josephine pulled out was his wallet. The hospital gave it to her after he died, and she had put it in the trunk. She looked through it and took out a few pieces of paper. They must have been important because she put them in her purse. Pat said he wanted the wallet so Josephine took out the rest of the papers and gave it to him. As we looked through those papers, Josephine told us stories about different things: receipts from places they had lived in Chicago, old insurance slips, check stubs, and business cards for lawyers, probably from times he had been in jail and needed bail. There was also a piece of paper from *Reader's Digest,* saying that he is among the luckiest people in Lincoln to receive four lucky number certificates in the newest sweepstakes. The numbers had been torn off. Frank probably had sent them in, hoping this would be his ticket to easy street. This was something he seemed to be searching for all his life. I hoped he had found his easy street in heaven.

There was also a picture of Frank, a small, two-by-two-inch black and white picture, the kind taken in a dime store photo booth. I took these things and cherished these last little pieces I had of my daddy. Frank had been the strength in our family. Now the only strength we had left was each other. So we dried our tears and put away our sorrow while trying to stand on shaky legs and find a new path.

When school ended in May, we moved to downtown Lincoln. Here we were closer to the job Pat got at a grocery store. He did pretty well with that and seemed to enjoy it. He brought me sheets of white oval stickers from the store. I put them on my fingers and pretended I had long, beautiful, white nails.

Josephine also had a couple of jobs. The first was washing dishes for a small restaurant on O Street. It was a small place with only a bar and stools for people to sit on. The back work area was also cramped. There was no air-conditioning so it was hot from the cooking, baking, and hot water used to wash the dishes. I often went with Josephine to work, but I stayed outside in the back, amusing myself with whatever discarded things I could find. As I watched her through the screen door, she often looked hot and tired as she stood by the sink, her arms in water up to her elbows.

After that job, she worked in a commercial laundry near O and 24th. I wasn't allowed to go with her there. This place was definitely more dangerous for children. There were huge machines with lids that lifted up and down. Garments were laid on the flat surface, and the lid was put down. As it pressed the garment, super-hot steam barreled from all sides. Machines with big rollers flattened the clothes and squeezed out water. It was hot and loud in this place. The big, noisy machines scared me, and the heat made it hard to breathe. I don't think Josephine liked this job either. But she was working and earning money so things were starting to look up for our family.

The three of us had some fun times also. A couple of times we went to the Pershing Center, a multi-purpose arena in Lincoln. We went to an all-star wresting event and a car show. One car at the show was called the Golden Sahara. This car for the future could do the driving for you. The big advantage of it, at least from Pat's thinking, was that if you were too drunk to drive home, the car could get you there. This was 1969, and it was supposed to come out in 1990. For me that seemed like an eternity away.

Things were going fine for a while, but soon Josephine got tired of working such difficult, labor-intensive jobs. She hadn't worked while Frank was alive, so the stress of working to make a living, along with her need for alcohol and a desire to "party" (her word for sex), as well as the instability Frank's death brought into our family, was too much for her.

Josephine started going to bars again and taking us with her.

I remember one of the first times we went to a bar with Josephine. It was strange being there without Frank. The bar was downtown, and I didn't remember ever going there before. We didn't know anyone else, and it felt awkward. Then a man came up and started talking to Josephine. I guess he was trying to pick her up. What kind of loser would try to pick up a woman in a bar with her two children sitting there?

He was trying to be cool and smooth as he talked to her. She smiled and tried to look pretty. Pat and I just looked at each other. We rolled our eyes at this stupid situation. What our mother and this guy were doing, right there in front of us, was disgusting and creepy. Who wants to hear some stranger talk dirty to your mom while you're sitting right there?

Finally, Pat and I stared at him. To this point, he had been ignoring us while he talked to Josephine. Our staring made him uncomfortable, and he left. Thankfully, Pat and I had scared this guy off, but a new chapter started in the life of our family: guys Josephine picked up in bars came home with us. I don't think it was many, but there were a few. Pat and I hated this. How could she put us through this? How could she do this to Daddy's memory so soon after he was gone?

It wasn't too long until she finally stuck with one guy, John. Now he was at our home all the time. He slept over a lot, but I don't think he ever moved in. However, along with John came his nephews who hung around too. I had more unsafe males to deal with. More males drinking, smoking, and eating what little food we had in the house. More males that I had to be on alert with and to keep myself safe around. When Frank was alive, I only had to deal with him and Pat, but now Frank was not there to keep things from getting out of control.

Pat did not keep things under control. When these guys made lewd comments or tried to grope me, he joined in. This only added to my fear and insecurity. He became friends with them and then brought other friends home. So now I had to deal with Josephine's boyfriends and all the family that came with them, plus Pat's new friends. When Frank was alive, I don't remember Pat having any friends, at least none he brought home. Now my life was becoming very complicated. When a female, no matter what age, lives in a world of sexually perverted males, she has to always be on alert in order to stay safe. I was still nine when all this started.

I have no memory of my tenth birthday or anything we may have done as a family to celebrate. (When my own daughters turned ten, we made a big deal out of them coming into double digits. We had a party with their friends and grandparents. They got to pick what kind of cake they wanted and what to have for dinner. I have great memories and pictures of each of my daughters' tenth birthdays but none of my own.)

I imagine Josephine remembered my birthday because she usually did. We probably went to a bar or maybe a restaurant that served alcohol and ate supper there. Josephine wanted to do something nice for me and thought I would enjoy what she enjoyed. Our family knew few ways to celebrate except going to bars.

So my tenth birthday came and went, and life continued to become crazy and out of control. I had to figure out how to care for myself and keep myself safe because my mother wasn't doing a good job of it. I felt safer being by myself than with my family.

Early that summer, it became apparent I needed an operation. I often had trouble with sore throats and swollen glands. Over the years doctors had noticed a small lump in my neck that now had gotten bigger. Finally, a doctor said it had to come out. He said if it weren't removed, it might eventually grow so large it would affect my vocal chords and my ability to talk. This may have been true or it may have been a way to force my mother to get me the surgery I had needed for years.

It wasn't a major operation, but I had to be in the hospital for a couple of days. Josephine and John took me to Lincoln General Hospital. The nurse gave me a bath and clean pajamas when I first got there. Never having been in a hospital before, I thought this was normal. For years I thought everyone took a bath and was given pajamas after arriving at the hospital. But now, as an adult who has been to the hospital several times, I know this isn't true. It was because of my circumstances. I'm sure I was dirty most of the time. I had long brown hair, and it always had tangles in it. I could never totally comb through it.

The surgery was scary. I remember my arms being stretched out and strapped down on the table. I looked over at my right arm and saw a huge needle sticking in it. The nurses were getting everything ready, but no one was talking to me, telling me what was happening. Finally, someone put a cloth over my eyes and said, "Okay, it's time to go to sleep." They put something over my mouth and nose that smelled awful. I started shaking my head back and forth trying to get them to stop and take the horrible thing off me. Soon I was asleep.

Other than the actual surgery, I really enjoyed being in the hospital. I was alone most of the time, and it was clean. The hospital was a safe place because none of Josephine's boyfriends or Pat's friends were around. There was good food to eat and TV to watch.

Josephine and John did come to visit but not a lot. There could have been many reasons for their absence. Maybe they didn't want to come or didn't know they should be there. Perhaps they didn't have transportation to get to the hospital. Maybe the hospital staff discouraged them from coming because of their drinking and smoking. Whatever the reasons, I was happy to be by myself and to be cared for by the nurses.

Now, as an adult, I realize how abnormal that hospital stay was in terms of parental involvement. It's sad to say that I felt safer there with strangers then I did at home. The truth was Josephine was drinking a lot, and the men and older boys in the house made my own home a very uncomfortable place for me.

Even before Frank's death, the fabric of our family had always been stretched tight; it would not take much for the cloth to tear and our family to fall apart. Now the seams were starting to rip, and one by one the stitches were popping.

Chapter 10
Unsafe Environments

Because Josephine was hanging out with her boyfriends, I started spending more and more time with Pat and his friends. Taking me along was cramping her style with the men. She was dating again after being married for many years. She was having fun drinking with her new boyfriends, and she didn't want me coming along. So I was left to fend for myself or go with Pat.

Being with Pat and his friends was an unsafe place for me. They did some bad things. One of the worst was with a naive and unsuspecting teenage Mary.

This whole horrible event started when Mary would not have sex with any of the guys; she would not "put out," as I heard them say. This confused and frustrated these boys. In their eyes, there was no other reason for females to exist. There was only one reason to associate with girls, and that was to have sex with them. But Mary wasn't playing their game. To make matters worse, she wouldn't even pair off with one of the guys. If she had done that, at least the boys would have had the satisfaction that someone was getting something. Then when one guy was done with her, they would pass her around. That would at least give the other guys hope.

I don't believe Mary understood this perverted view of women and the kind of twisted sexual belief these young men held to. She didn't realize how unsafe it was for her to not be attached to one guy. When, as a female, you are viewed only as sexual property, it is best to belong to someone. But Mary didn't belong to anyone. She just wanted to have friends. She thought her acceptance in this group was purely friendship. She failed to realize that they saw her only as a walking vagina.

I don't know how long it took the boys to realize Mary wasn't going to put out. When they did, the plan began. Because I was always left in the care of my brother, I was in on much of the planning.

They decided the place would be Oak Park. This was a large park with a lake. It wasn't in a residential part of Lincoln but close to the end of town, surrounded by industrial buildings. As a hangout and party place for teenagers, it was an ideal location because I'm sure alcohol, drugs, and sex flowed freely there.

After they chose where, they had to choose when. A weeknight would be best. On a weekend night too many people might be around. They couldn't take a chance on being seen or heard. So the day was decided: a Tuesday night. The fact that it was a school night made no difference to them.

After that, the only thing left was to figure out how. So they began making decisions about where to go in the park, choosing the darkest, most secluded place. Would they put her on the ground or in the backseat of the car? Whose car would they take? Rob's seemed like the best choice. But no, that wouldn't work. It was a small, two-door '65 Mustang, and they would need a large backseat. This planning stage also decided who would rip off her clothes and who would go first.

They talked about tearing off her panties and tossing them over the roof of the car. Pat and Rob were the masterminds, but they brought in a couple of other friends for the big night.

When it finally arrived, I did not want to go, but I had no choice. Josephine had plans that didn't include me. We took the big car with the large backseat and picked up this innocent, unsuspecting girl from her house. She willingly got into the car, thinking she was going out for a fun evening with her friends. She always seemed happy and eager to be with them. Unfortunately, this poor girl had no idea what was in store for her.

We went to the park. The sun had already set, and darkness filled the sky. There were a lot of trees and picnic tables and a large shelter house right next to the lake. It was an early October evening in Nebraska, so the air was cool. Everyone got out of the car and stood around talking. Someone brought beer, stolen from his parents' fridge. Maybe there was a bottle of hard liquor and, of course, there were cigarettes. Everyone smoked. I don't remember them ever doing drugs, except for one guy who sniffed model airplane glue. He always stank of the stuff, and I hated to be around him.

Rob was probably the one to initiate the asking. That was the way sexual abuse always started with these guys. Their approach started with pushing the boundaries, getting too close, asking too much. "Come on, baby, give me a kiss. Come on, let me touch you." Mary probably gave in initially because she wanted to be nice; they were all friends, or at least that's what she thought. But when they started asking for more than she was comfortable with, and she resisted, that's when they believed they were justified to get mean, to force her, and become violent.

I stood back, watching this whole thing unfold. I was seeing a horrible event and I wanted to turn away, but I just kept watching, knowing what was going to happen. When she resisted, she thought she had a choice.

As things got worse and the violence against this poor girl escalated, I couldn't watch any longer and walked away. But I was only able to go a short distance from the car and the horror. I wanted to walk out of the park and to a safe place. Unfortunately, there was no place like that in my life. Even if I would have had the courage to walk away and go home, it was miles and miles to my house. I knew the way, but I didn't know who I would meet along the way. I knew this horrible situation, and I thought I could handle it. Alone on the streets of Lincoln, a worse fate might await me.

Another reason I didn't leave was because Pat and his friends would be mad at me if I left. They would have to come after me. If Pat came home without me, our mother might ask too many questions. I knew it was not safe to make them mad because, just like tonight with Mary, when you made them mad, that gave them the right to attack. I was terrified that they would attack me also. The only way I knew to keep myself safe was to not make them mad.

So I walked away as far as I could, terrified with what was happening. I didn't want to hear it, didn't want to be part of it, so I stayed away. No one missed me anyway, and I was glad to be invisible to them. I was not the main course that night. I don't know how long it took. When the screams and the cursing stopped, I walked back to the car. Mary was sitting in the car, unclothed, shaking and crying. I remained silent and sat next to her. She was beside the door. I was in the middle and one of them was beside me, but I don't remember who. As she continued to cry, she held on to me with both arms. She thought I was safe, that I was on her side. I patted her arms as a gesture of comfort, but I didn't dare say anything. I didn't dare because if the boys knew I sided with her they might turn on me.

But I did side with Mary. I hated what had happened to

her, but I also felt partly to blame. I knew what was going to happen, but I didn't tell anyone. I was sitting there trying to comfort her, but I hadn't warned her. I felt guilty and ashamed. Mary, the victim of rape, was in no way to blame for what had happened to her.

I couldn't let the boys know my true feelings; they thought I was on their side. The small part I played in this horrible night made me sad and ashamed. But even as a ten-year-old, I knew that keeping myself safe was most important. Using my mind to figure out how to manipulate these guys so they wouldn't get mad at me, so they also wouldn't hurt me, was what I needed to do. Staying safe was the only thing I could really worry about. My home was an emotional war zone with enemies all around. I could not rely on others for help; I had to figure things out by myself.

Another unsafe time for me was one night with Pat and his friends at the apartment of a man named Bobo. This probably was not his real name, and I have no idea what it stood for. He was a friend of Marvin's, the man Josephine was with at the time. I think Marvin knew Bobo from working on the garbage truck.

Bobo wasn't a horrible person. He was weird and creepy, not someone a child should be left alone with, but he wasn't mean or angry. Neither was he a safe adult who would protect me. He acted the same as the sex-crazed teenage boys I hung with.

One night Pat and I and two or three of Pat's friends were at Bobo's apartment. They were drinking beer and smoking. Then one of the boys got the idea to play a game. They decided on strip poker. In this abusive environment, my alert level to keep myself safe was always an orange, inching up to red. However, when I heard what they wanted to play, my alert level shot up to red and higher.

I was alone in an apartment with several sexually perverted

men who had been drinking, and I knew how dangerous they were. My brain kicked into a primitive mode. It was the fight or flight response, but I could do neither. There was no place to go, and I was not going to do anything that would anger them; this would have definitely brought violence against me.

I had no choice but to play along. How could I play strip poker with them but also keep myself safe? I had to pretend it was no problem playing this game with them. Resisting, showing weakness, or letting them know how scared I was could have been worse for me.

Finally, after the first round or so, I got my strategy for staying safe. Their goal was for my clothes to come off, and my goal was to keep my clothes on. It was winter, so everyone had brought coat, gloves, scarf, and hat. These were either hung up or lying around the room. When it was someone else's turn to play, I'd walk around the room and put on their items of clothing. That way I had plenty of clothes to take off.

For some reason, to which only God knows the answer, this stunt did not anger them. I tried to keep it light and funny and never let them know how scared I was. They finally got tired, and we quit playing.

Many bad things happened with Pat and his friends, including more sexual abuse and molestation against me, but these two situations were the worst. What I did not realize at the time was what living in constant fear and stress was doing to my brain. I had no place to go for help, no safe person to process these horrible events with and so these traumas kept piling up in my life and brain. This changed the way my brain developed and would permanently affect the way I viewed the world and the way I felt the world viewed me.

I didn't think I could tell anyone about this and expect the person to do anything. Behavior like this had become so much a part of my life that I didn't fully understand how wrong and abnormal it was. I didn't like it, but I didn't think there was hope for anything different. Such behavior was all I knew.

Up to this point, no one had done anything to change my life. No one seemed to care when our family was homeless and lived in the condemned house on Leighton for several months. No one had done anything permanent when I almost passed out in the third grade because I was hungry. If no one cared about my poverty and hunger, why would they care about the sexual abuse that was happening to me? There seemed to be no point in telling anyone.

Chapter 11
Running Away

"That ain't true. Nobody'd do that," Pat said. We were sitting at the kitchen table.

"N-n-n-no, it's really true. I found 'em layin right there on t-t-t-top of the garbage can. A whole carton of Marlboros," said Marvin, the man Josephine was living with.

To say Marvin was creepy would be an understatement. His mouth turned up at the ends in what should have been a smile, but it only seemed to magnify his creepiness. He tried to be cool and suave, but he wasn't. His hair was black and always slicked back with grease. His nose was small and pointy, his eyes like slits. He could look out through them, but he didn't want others to see inside. He was somewhat handsome, but from looking at him, you could tell he was not a good person.

We were sitting around the table after supper, and he was bragging to Josephine about the great things he had found working on the garbage truck.

"But that's just stupid. Why would anyone throw away

a whole carton of cigarettes?" Pat said. In his world this did seem unbelievable. "You're a f——in' liar," Pat blurted out. He wasn't looking at Marvin directly, but he didn't say it under his breath either.

"Patrick!" Josephine snapped in an effort to reprimand him for talking to Marvin that way. Pat ignored her. She didn't have any parental authority over him anymore. Pat was seventeen. He had taken on the role as man of the house after Frank died. Now Josephine had brought in Marvin, and the two were always in conflict. Pat saw Marvin as a rival. So added to the insanity in our home with alcohol and no sexual boundaries, testosterone wars waged. I wouldn't have been surprised to see them peeing on the furniture to mark their territory.

Next Marvin spoke up. "Now, s-s-s-son, don't use that kind of language in front of your mom and sis." He was trying to impress Josephine by sounding concerned, but the truth was I heard him use much worse language when he was

Josephine and Marvin

drunk. Also, he mistakenly thought he could parent us. But I had given up any hope of my mother parenting me, and I certainly wasn't going to let this jerk come in and be my new "Daddy Marvin."

"Don't call me 'son.' I'm not your son. Just 'cause you're screwin' my mom don't make you my dad," Pat yelled.

"Now, son, you just s-s-s-settle down," Marvin said, his stutter becoming more pronounced.

"I said I'm not your son." Pat lunged at him in an attempt to hit him in the face. But Marvin quickly moved out of the way. Josephine tried to hold Pat back, but he pushed her off. She stumbled back. This angered Marvin. He grabbed a butcher knife from the table and pointed it at Pat.

At first I couldn't believe what was happening. The fear of what Marvin might do to Pat was more than I thought I could handle. The violence I had experienced had always been physical, but never with weapons. I didn't know how to handle someone with a knife. As these thoughts raced in my mind, I worried he would kill Pat and then turn the knife on me and my mom.

Marvin didn't attack; he waved the knife around, telling Pat to get out. Then we both looked at Josephine. What would she do? What would she say? She had never been strong except when she was drunk. She was not drunk now. and she just sat there. This was a clear message to us that she was not going to stand up to Marvin and protect her children. As Pat walked out the door, he turned to me and yelled, "Come on, Kathy."

I ran out with him. If I had a choice between Pat and my mother, then there was really no choice. I loved my mother, but I didn't respect her. She was weak. She drank too much and acted stupid when she was drunk. Pat was not a great choice for someone to protect me and keep me safe, but he was much better than my mom.

Pat and I ran away from home on a freezing cold night in February 1970. We walked because there was no car to take. We wore only light jackets; there hadn't been enough time to look for heavier clothing. We had a long walk ahead of us. Our destination was Aunt Dona's house. She was the one everyone in our family went to when they needed help as we did that night.

We lived on 20th, just off of J Street, and we walked to O Street. O is the main east-west street in Lincoln. That stretch was the shortest part of our journey. After we reached O Street, we turned east and had many miles to go.

Pat had a friend who worked at a gas station on O Street. We stopped there to warm up. He gave us some hot cocoa and coffee to drink. Pat had hoped to wait until he got off work, but that was several hours away, and I sensed the guy didn't want to help us. However, we were thankful for the break and warm drink before starting on our way again.

After we had walked several more blocks, Pat stuck out his thumb to hitchhike. It wasn't long before someone picked us up and drove us part way to Havelock, a small suburb on the east edge of Lincoln, where Dona lived. He dropped us off several miles from her house. Thankfully, Dona had a sister, Teresa, who lived on the edge of Havelock. We went there.

It was late, around 10 p.m. We were cold, tired, and frightened when we got to Teresa's house, but she welcomed us in. We spent the night there, and in the morning Dona came and got us.

We spent several days with Aunt Dona as she tried to figure out what to do with us. She called social services, and someone came out and talked to us about what happened with Josephine and Marvin. However, social services did not feel our situation was bad enough to remove us from the home.

Dona also took us out to where Grandma Sekoris lived. She was a very old woman and lived by herself in Prague, a town several miles from Lincoln. Because of her age, she wasn't really a good solution for us. Also, she was Frank's mother, and she hated our mother. I don't think she felt any real responsibility to take care of us. We were not her biological grandchildren, and she didn't want to have any connection with our mother now that her son was dead.

Grandma Sekoris had always been nice to me, and I loved her. I thought she loved me too. When she said she would not take us in, I cried. What was going to happen to us? We had tried to keep ourselves safe by getting away from Marvin and Josephine, but now no one would take care of us.

Finally, the decision was made. Because Pat was in the most danger from Marvin, he would not go back. They sent him off to join Dona's husband, Arkie. He ran a carnival, and Pat could work for him. There was really nothing to hold him to Lincoln other than me. He had dropped out of high school by this point. Keeping me safe was less important than his safety. So Pat left, and I was sent back to our mother and Marvin.

Seeing Pat leave was the worst thing I had ever experienced in my life. How was I going to survive without him? I didn't want to go back into this crazy situation, but I had no choice. I was only a child, and the adults made all the decisions for me. I don't think any of them thought this was a good choice, but there really wasn't any other one.

Chapter 12
Alone with Josephine

It had been less than a year since Frank died, and now Pat was gone. What little safety and security I felt in my life was quickly dissolving.

I was on my own because Josephine would not or could not keep me safe. She was weak and seemed to have absolutely no power in her life. Perhaps she got mean when she drank because this was the only time she felt power. But it was a power based on nothing. She was powerless to her addictions, to her poverty, and to her lack of skills and resources. The anger that came out when alcohol lowered her inhibitions was directed at that powerlessness, and that was destroying her life. It was also destroying my life even though I knew Josephine loved me.

Her anger was rarely directed at me. Usually it was directed at the men in her life, first Frank and now Marvin. Still, the anger scared me; I never knew what she would do or how far she would go.

Kathy at age 10

One night the anger directed at Marvin went pretty far. Marvin was not like Frank. Frank could and did control her rage. I had felt safer when he was there because he would not let Josephine go too far. But Marvin was different, Josephine's anger intimidated him. One particular night they had been to a bar; both came home drunk.

"Why the hell did you do that? What the f—— were you thinking?" Josephine screeched at Marvin as we were standing in the kitchen.

"I don't know. I'm s-o-o-o sorry, sweetie. It-t-t-t'll never happen agin." Marvin slurred his words, looking defeated like a wounded puppy.

"I don't want to catch you looking at that little whore again. Do you hear me, you mother——er?"

Marvin continued to stand there, mumbling over and over again, "I'm sorry, I'm so sorry, sweetie." Then Josephine took her shoe off. Oh, good, I thought, she's done and now she's getting undressed to go to bed.

But I was wrong. She took her shoe, which had a three-inch spiked heel and starting beating him on the side of his head.

"Do you want to be with that slut, you asshole? Is that what you want?" *POW, POW, POW.* She continued nailing him in the head with her shoe. She smacked the heel into his left temple as blood ran down the side of his face.

"No, honey. I'm sorry, I'm so sorry," Marvin mumbled.

"Do you want to leave me for that slut? You drove my boy away. Do you want to leave me too, you son of a bitch?"

Marvin stopped talking and stood there crying. Then as the blood continued down his face, he stumbled back and fell against the fridge. This may have been because of the alcohol or he was losing consciousness from of the beating. Whatever it was, it broke Josephine's rage. She stopped hitting him, threw her shoe to the floor, and walked to her bedroom.

Marvin slid to the floor with his back against the fridge. I ran back to Pat's room, in the back of the house, which had a door to the outside. I felt safer knowing I had an escape, hoping no one would come after me. I sat on his bed and waited to see what would happen.

While they were fighting, neither Marvin nor Josephine seemed to know I was there. Hopefully they would not realize I was gone now. I didn't want Marvin to come looking for me after Josephine passed out. Maybe he would do to me what he didn't have the courage to do to Josephine. He might try to exert power over me, either physically or sexually. Thankfully, he did not come after me that night.

Even though I was not physically assaulted that night, I still suffered trauma from this experience. One adult had viciously beat up another adult, and neither seemed to care that a ten-year-old was watching the whole thing. My trauma was the extreme fear I felt because of how out of control these two adults were in their violence. I was terrified of what they would do to each other or what they would do to me. There were many other scary, yucky things in that house. One night either Marvin or Josephine was smoking in bed, and the mattress caught fire. They carried it out in the middle of the night. I woke the next morning to the smell of smoke and saw the smoldering remains in the backyard.

Cockroaches infested the house. Whenever I opened a drawer to get silverware, the cockroaches scattered. Somehow a cockroach managed to get into my ear and die. I have no idea when this happened, but one morning while I was at mass before school, my ear was itching, so I scratched it. As I felt in the top rim of my ear, I pulled out a dead, dry cockroach skin. At the time I thought it was pretty cool. Now, forty years later, I realize the extent of the filth in which I was forced to live.

The house was extremely messy. Our houses were always filled with stuff. Josephine was a hoarder. The hoard had come from treasures found on our trips to the dump. Now that Frank was gone, we didn't go to the dumps anymore, so maybe she had brought the hoard with her or maybe it was Marvin's stuff that he had not unpacked after moving in. Whatever the reason, that house seemed to be the worst. The walls were lined with stuff. Stuff in boxes, stuff on the floor. Even Playboy magazines lying around that no one cared to keep private.

However, in this houseful of stuff no one could find a shower curtain to hang up. The bathroom was disgusting. The tub didn't have a stopper for the drain so there was no way to take a bath. The tub was too dirty to even think about that. Still, I remember showering in there, probably making a watery mess on the floor, but I didn't care about that. And I always kept my underwear on when I was showering to keep myself safe in case anyone walked in on me.

Not only was the house filthy, but depressing. It was not

a home. My whole family was not there, just my powerless, alcoholic mom and the stranger she lived with. I missed my stepfather a lot, but even more I missed Pat. In many ways he had been my best friend throughout childhood. Because he was my older brother, he had been there all my life. I had never been alone with the crazy adults in our life until now. I felt very alone.

Josephine had left Pat's room the way it was when he left. Sometimes I would go back there and just sit. I would look at all the model cars he had put together. Hobbies were not a big thing in our lives, but this was his hobby. He was good at it and proud of his cars. They were a part of him, and now they seemed to be the only part I had left. I would sit with the cars and cry, wishing my brother would come back home.

Most of the time in that house, Josephine's moods seemed to be at two extremes. After drinking, she was either angry or quiet. I remember her sitting on the front porch, just staring. I tried to talk to her, but she didn't respond much. She sat there and stared as she puffed on her cigarette. Now, as an adult, I realize she probably suffered from severe depression.

However, there was a happier memory for Josephine and me during that time. At Josephine's insistence, I had my singing debut in Lincoln. I had always enjoyed singing. Josephine encouraged this because she told me that she sang in bars when she was younger. She had been twenty, and not ten like me, but this was something we bonded over.

One popular song during the early 1970s was "Harper Valley PTA." I sang along with the radio when this song played, and I learned all the words.

One day when I was at a bar with Josephine and Marvin, someone played this song on the jukebox. I sat quietly and sang along with it as I always did.

"Kathy, why don't you get up and sing?" Marvin asked.

"No, I don't want to do that." I suddenly felt shy and didn't want to be pressured into doing something I didn't want to do.

"Oh, Kathy, that's a great idea." Josephine said. "You could get up there and sing that song. Marvin, go and play it again on the jukebox."

So Marvin got up and went to the jukebox, put in a quarter and punched the number for the song. Little did I know that he punched the number for "Harper Valley PTA" three times. That's how many songs a quarter could buy.

The song started again, and Josephine and Marvin coaxed me to get up and sing. Marvin stood by the jukebox and motioned for me to come over, and Josephine tried to push me out of my seat at the table. Others in the bar looked, and this encouraged Marvin to announce to the whole bar, "We have a star here today, and she's goin' sing for us."

Then everyone looked at me. The truth was I did love singing that song, so I got up, stood by the jukebox, and sang.

At first I sang quietly, and then as I got more comfortable, I sang louder. By the time the song came around for the third time, I was really singing and even walking around to the tables and booths in the bar. As I did this, people put money on the table, just a couple of coins, but I was excited.

I picked up the coins and moved on. When I got to the bar, a couple of men picked me up and sat me on the bar. I finished the song sitting there. It was great fun.

I remember doing this a time or two more at this place and then at another bar. I always got a little money from the people listening, and Josephine let me keep it. Before, when Pat or I had gotten money for Christmas or a birthday, Frank and Josephine talked us into giving it to them.

They said we needed it to buy food or go out somewhere to eat. But this time I got to keep the money, and I bought toys with it at the dime store.

This was a positive experience for me on a couple of levels. First, I felt valued by Josephine and Marvin. I was doing something I was good at and enjoyed. Plus, it made them happy. Also, this song really spoke to Josephine. It was about an unmarried mom, considered wild by the other PTA mothers. This judgment made her daughter feel ashamed of herself and her mom. But the mother went to the PTA meeting and confronted the other mothers. She told them of their sins or the sins of their husbands with other women and vindicated herself and her daughter.

I'm sure Josephine felt shamed by the other parents at St. Mary's, the Catholic school I attended, so she could identify with the mother in the song. She probably wished she had the courage to confront those who judged her. My singing this song was a kind of validation for her and a way for us to identify with each other.

I felt torn between my love for my mother and my desire for a different life. I didn't like the way she lived and the things she was doing. I wanted her to be a normal PTA mom. Just like the song, I wanted her to be different.

Chapter 13
"God, I Need a Miracle"

The one bright spot in my life during this time was school. I had not always enjoyed school and usually tried to get out of it whenever I could. That year, however, I don't remember missing as much school. One reason was that it was worse to be at home than in school. The other reason was my teacher, Mrs. Johnson. She was the only teacher I had had up to this point that I felt really saw me and not the poverty and crap I lived in. She saw that I was a bright little girl living in difficult circumstances. In fact, when Josephine went to a parent-teacher conference, Mrs. Johnson told her I could be the smartest student in the class if I only tried a little harder. I felt proud, and I think Josephine did too.

Because I had been in different schools every year and because of the trauma in my life, I had difficulty focusing. I was not up to grade levels in some areas so Mrs. Johnson arranged for me to have a tutor.

My tutor was an elementary education student from the University of Nebraska. She was young and pretty and very nice. However, I was not always as kind to her. I felt safe and comfortable with her and could just be a kid. During our tutoring sessions, I messed around, grabbing her pencil and throwing it across the room or other stuff just to fool around. I didn't do anything mean; I just wanted to have fun somewhere in my life, and she was a safe person.

I remember going to study in her dorm room at the university and meeting some of her friends. I did not know anyone else who went to college and had such cool friends. Her life gave me a glimpse into what I wanted my life to look like. At that time, it seemed like an impossible dream that I could ever go to college and become a teacher like my tutor. Without even knowing it, they planted a seed in my heart and mind, a seed that would eventually grow and bear fruit.

The other positive thing about St. Mary's School was a girl named Sarah. She was in my class and, like me, also an outcast. She was shy, lacked confidence, was overweight and an easy target for bullies. But she was nice to me and seemed to need and want my friendship as badly as I needed hers.

I remember one school project was to start a business. Sarah and I were partners. I had the idea of making posters, and she went along with it. I had seen the movie "Bonnie and Clyde" (hardly a movie for a child), and so I made poster using their pictures. We had some other, more fourth-grade appropriate ones as well. Our little posters were not as popular as the green Jell-O bugs some kids made, but we had fun. School and projects like this were the only normal age-appropriate things I had in my life that year.

Another good thing about this school was going to mass every morning before school started. I also went through catechism that year. I don't know if they asked me if I wanted to take it or if all the fourth graders were in it. We went to separate classes and learned more about the Bible than we did in school. The main thing I remember were the prayers: Our Father, Hail Mary, and the Apostle's Creed.

The Apostle's Creed stood out the most for me, especially the part that said Jesus "suffered under Pontius Pilate, was crucified, died and was buried. He descended into hell; on the third day he rose again from the dead; he ascended into heaven and is seated at the right hand of the Father." (The Cathechism of the Catholic Church)

Jesus had suffered greatly and was even in hell. I could relate to this. I was suffering, too.

This was the first time I understood about Jesus dying on the cross and what that meant and also, that a miracle had happened in his life: He rose from the dead. I needed a miracle too. Would believing in Jesus bring me one? I knew if my life was going to be saved, I needed something bigger than me. I needed God. So I accepted what they were teaching me and hung on to that hope, the belief that God would save me.

This hope for a miracle came about in an interesting way one Sunday afternoon and involved my favorite food, candy. There was a Russell Stover candy factory in Lincoln at the time. I had often passed it and longingly looked at the display candy in the window. As a kid, I never realized this candy was only for display and not real.

One Sunday afternoon when I again had to stay with Bobo, he told me he had a special treat for me. When he showed me the box of candy, I was overjoyed. Wow, here was a whole box of candy, this wonderful candy I had so often seen in the factory window, and it was for me. But as I took a piece from the box and tried to take that first yummy, sweet bite, I was sadly disappointed. I kept trying, thinking maybe the candy was a little old and the outer coating was hard. But I soon understood something was very wrong with this candy.

When Bobo realized that I had figured out this wasn't normal candy, he laughed. He told me it was fake candy used only for display, and he had found it in the trash. Gross! He had found it in the trash, and I was putting it in my mouth! Then I felt sad. What I thought was going to be a wonderful treat was just another lie.

That whole afternoon I couldn't accept the idea that this candy wasn't real. I sat there looking at it, thinking that if I just looked hard enough and believed strong enough, the candy would become real. It did not, but I never forgot that candy.

What I wanted was a miracle. For the fake candy to become real would truly have been a miracle. However, the miracle I needed and wanted was not about candy at all. It was about my life and my family. I wanted to have a family again. I wanted Pat to come home and Josephine to strengthen up and be my mom. This was the miracle I needed. I wanted to be safe, loved, and valued by the adults in my life.

I did not know it then, but, looking back, I believe that God was there with me that afternoon. God gave me the ability to keep hoping, the ability to pray for a miracle. Even though the miracle would not come that day, God was whispering in my ear, "Keep going; the good will come. One day you will be safe and loved and have all these things you long for now. The hard times are not over. Hang on a little longer; there is hope. And remember, I am here walking beside you."

As school ended and summer came, I carried with me this hope for a miracle, this hope in God. Josephine and I continued to walk further and further down the valley of the shadow of death, but I had a new tool to help me. This new tool was my hope in a higher power. The prayers I learned in catechism also comforted me. They gave me a sense of protection. I said these prayers at night when I was scared about what would happen. Lying in bed, I said the prayers to comfort and protect myself.

The summer started out with Marvin and Josephine still together. The three of us moved into a trailer park. The trailer was dumpy but no worse than most of the houses we had lived in. I had never lived in a trailer, and I thought it was cool.

The level of tension between Josephine and Marvin was rising, and not only did I have to live with this tension, but I also felt I was partly to blame for it. I continued to be uncomfortable around him. One time we went to a bar and he wanted me to dance with him. He kept coaxing me even though I didn't want to dance. Refusing him didn't seem like a solution because he'd probably get mad at me. So I agreed. Dancing with him made me feel embarrassed. I tried to not move my body much. Doing this might give him or the other guys in the bar the wrong idea. They might think I was trying to be sexy, and I definitely didn't want to give them that idea.

My mother didn't like Marvin giving me so much attention. She was getting mad, more at him than at me. I was put in the position of pleasing one adult while making the other one angry. Because they were both basically crazy and even more crazy and violent when they were drinking, I didn't know what to do or what they might do. But I danced with him that night, and I don't remember anything horrible happening when we got home.

As things got worse between them, Marvin and Josephine finally broke up. Early that summer of 1970 Josephine and I became homeless. It didn't last long, but the memory of it was powerful for me. I'm sure it was powerful because with all that I had lost, even the small security I had in a home was gone. I had no hope in Josephine being able to care for us.

Another thing at that time that made me feel exposed was that I didn't have any underwear. I had been swimming with some kids from a family we knew. I had to borrow a bathing suit from one of the girls and, of course, you don't wear underwear with a bathing suit. After we were done swimming, I had to give the swimming suit back. When I went to put my clothes on, my underwear was missing, so I had to put on my shorts with no underwear. I remember hating that feeling. I felt exposed and vulnerable. I felt uncomfortable because I did not have the security of something as basic as underwear. I had to be very aware of how I walked, how I sat, who was looking at me, and if they knew I wasn't wearing any underwear.

I don't know why we couldn't go back to our trailer, but we couldn't, not even to get my underwear. Maybe Josephine couldn't pay the rent and we were kicked out of the trailer. Maybe she was hiding from Marvin or John, the two primary men in her life. It could have been one of these or any number of crazy reasons for our homelessness. But I remember it being a scary time.

Other things made Josephine and me vulnerable. We didn't have a place to stay, not even a car to sleep in. I don't think the rescue mission would have taken a woman and a child. For some reason Josephine had chosen not to call Aunt Dona for help. So we were at the mercy of the people around us. At that time in my life there were not a lot of people around me who had good moral character or with whom I felt safe.

Josephine and I were at the bottom of the barrel. We had no money, not even enough to buy a pair of used underwear at the thrift store. We had no means of getting money. I was just a child, and Josephine didn't have a job and she couldn't drive. The only money we got was from the state: welfare checks and some social security from Frank. It was probably the end of the month so those funds were not yet available.

Also, we had no man—not a man to support us, although that would have been nice, but also no man to protect us. One thing I had learned in my ten years of living in this alcoholic, poverty-stricken culture was that it was better to have a man than not. And it was easier to manage one man than to have to fend off the perverted advances of many.

Living on the streets, we were alone and vulnerable with no home, no money, no man, and no protection. I thought this surely must be the bottom for us. Unfortunately, I was wrong.

Chapter 14
The Day Pat Came Back

After our brief period of homelessness, we moved back into our small trailer. One morning Josephine was sitting at the table, smoking a cigarette, and drinking coffee.

I yawned, stretched, and walked into the kitchen. Rubbing the sleep from my eyes, I sat down at the table. It was summer, which meant no school and sleeping late.

"Someone said Patrick is back," Josephine said.

The sleep cleared from my brain, and my eyes opened wide. The joy that started in my belly rose up through my body and ended in a huge smile.

"Where is he? Is he coming home?" I asked.

"No, he's not coming home. In California he hooked up with that oldest Jones boy, and he's stayin' with him." The hardness in Josephine's voice covered the sadness she felt that he wasn't coming home.

Josephine along with Marvin were to blame for Pat's leaving. Marvin had threatened him with a knife and kicked him out of the house the night we ran away. Josephine didn't defend us or stand up to Marvin. So she was just as much to blame. Even if she felt sorry for what she had done, I don't think she knew how to say she was sorry. This was just another way she didn't take personal responsibility for her actions. If she said she were sorry, then she would have to take the blame. But in her eyes she was never to blame. Other people always did stuff to her. She was always the victim.

"Can we go over and see him? I really want to see him," I pleaded.

"He doesn't want to see me. There's a party at Joe's tonight. You can go over and see him."

Joe lived down the block. I wanted to see Pat immediately. But the guy he was staying with lived too far away for me to go by myself, and Josephine wasn't going to take me. So I waited until evening and went to Joe's house by myself.

When I got there that evening, Pat was in the backyard, standing in a crowd of other people. Here was my best friend, my brother, and the only person in the world who I thought

Pat at age 17

loved me. I was filled with relief and joy when I first saw him. What I felt may have been like what a person feels when they have been kidnapped and finally their rescuer comes and takes them away. Here was my beloved brother, my only hope of some kind of salvation in my crazy life. I thought he had come back for me because I was his sister and he loved me. Here, standing in the cool summer evening, was the one person in the whole world I trusted.

He saw me and started walking toward me. I ran and threw my arms around him. He hugged me too. I don't know if it was at that moment or later when I realized something had changed. I was a master at reading people's emotions. Living with unstable alcoholics all my life gave me this skill. So it wasn't hard to read him. Slowly I understood he had not come to be with me and to be my family again. He had come only to visit, like strangers come and then leave. Only it wasn't a real visit, he didn't even come back to the trailer to have a meal with us. We just had a conversation in someone's backyard. He told me about the adventures he had with the carnival in California. He didn't seem to care much that I had had a horrible time without him, living with Josephine and Marvin.

Soon he had to leave. I wanted him to stay. I wanted to tell him all the things that had happened while he was gone. I wanted to talk to him all night. But, no, he had to go. Someone was waiting for him.

"Can I come with you?" I asked. Inside I was pleading, "Please, please, let me come."

He said no. He was staying with some other people and there wasn't room for me. "But I'll come back and see you," he said. At that moment I knew he had become another adult who promised things they would never deliver.

On that cool summer night I realized I was alone in the world. Frank, my stepfather, had died, Josephine had given her life to alcohol and men. Now Pat was gone. He was the person I trusted and cared most about in this world and who I thought loved and cared about me. However, he turned out to be like all the other crazy alcoholic adults in my life, concerned only with himself.

Pat gave me another hug and left. Sad, I walked back to our trailer. I lay in bed that night with tears streaming down my face. What was going to happen to me? Thankfully, God knew and had a plan.

Pat

Chapter 15
Where has Josephine Gone?

One Sunday afternoon in late June 1970, I was staying with some of Josephine's friends, Ellen and Richard. We were friends for a long time and I remember going there to play or for a meal. I liked playing with their two girls.

It was not a bad place to be and they were more stable than most of Josephine's friends. Of course, they got drunk with Josephine. Sometimes Ellen would get angry and hit her children and me if I happened to be close. Richard was less creepy then Marvin, but I didn't feel comfortable with him and never wanted to be close or alone with him. For my childhood, these people were pretty normal.

When I stayed with them this time, Josephine had to go somewhere for the afternoon. It was a normal, fun day. I played with the girls and tried to stay away from the adults. As evening came, I expected Josephine to come get me, but she didn't. It got dark, but no Josephine. Finally, Ellen told me my mom had something she needed to do, and she wouldn't be able to come that night so I should just stay with them. This didn't seem unusual, I had spent the night with them before, but what was weird is that Ellen was nicer to me than usual. I couldn't figure out the reason for this kindness, and that worried me more than Josephine's absence.

The next day Josephine still did not come, and Ellen was even nicer to me. When I asked her where my mom was and when she was coming to get me, Ellen said she had something to take care of and she'd be coming soon. I knew better than to push Ellen for information. I knew her sweetness could quickly turn to anger, and I didn't want to risk that. So I played most of that day, but as afternoon turned into evening and Josephine still had not appeared, I got very worried.

The next day I did not play. I sat on the front porch and looked down the street, hoping to see Josephine walking up the sidewalk. But she didn't come that day either. The longer Josephine was away, the nicer Ellen was to me, and this scared me. She knew where my mom was, but I didn't know why she wouldn't tell me. So my imagination was left to wonder. Maybe she had died like Frank or left me like Pat? What if she never came back?

Would I have to live with Ellen and Richard? These people were not my family; they didn't care for me the way Frank and Pat had and the way Josephine did. The only thing I had left was the sense that my mother loved me. Maybe that too was gone.

For the next two days I sat on Ellen's porch with these thoughts looping through my mind. Where was Josephine? Was she dead? Had she left me? Was she ever coming back? What would happen to me? My sadness and depression deepened.

Finally, I saw her walking down the sidewalk. I jumped up and ran to her, throwing my arms around her. I was so thankful she wasn't dead and that she hadn't left me. I was so thankful she was back so the fact that she had been in jail since Sunday night didn't bother me. It did bother me that Ellen knew where my mother was but hadn't told me.

"I thought your mother should be the one to tell you something like that," Ellen said when I asked her why she didn't tell me. Didn't she realize that the mental terror and anguish I experienced was much worse than any delicacy about who should tell me my mother was in jail? Knowing she was in jail would have been a welcome relief from thinking she had left me or was dead.

Chapter 16
Walking Around the Block

It was Friday night and Josephine had left me with Eddy and Sharon, the managers at the trailer park where we lived. They were about Josephine's age, maybe a little younger. When you're ten, everyone over twenty seems old. Their own children had been taken away from them by the state, but that didn't matter to me. I guess it didn't matter to Josephine either because she let me stay with them. Unlike many of the adults in my life, they were nice to me, and I didn't mind being around them.

We went to Harry's Bar on O Street. Being with them was not much different from being with Josephine. Their wants and desires came first. They had no problem going to a bar simply because they were babysitting a child for the weekend.

As we sat at a table in the bar, they drank beer and I had pop.

"Kathy, come back to the bathroom with me," Sharon said.

I didn't really need to use the bathroom, but I did as

she asked. I guess she didn't need to go either because as we walked down the hall she stopped me. "Kathy, would you like some pizza? They make a really good sausage and pepperoni one here."

"Sure," I said. My mouth started to water, and my stomach growled. "I would really like some pizza."

This was great, I thought. Sharon's going to get some pizza. We would actually have food with our pop and beer. Frank and Josephine rarely got food at bars. Even when Pat and I begged, they got mad and made us feel bad for asking. I had never been to a bar with Eddy and Sharon so maybe this was normal for them. Maybe they always got food at bars. However, I didn't understand why Sharon had asked me to come back to the bathroom with her and then asked me if I wanted pizza.

"Their pizza really is good here," she repeated. "Why don't you ask Eddy for some? I'm sure he'll get it for you. If I ask him, he'll say I'm too fat and don't need pizza." As Sharon continued to talk, my heart sank. She wasn't trying to be nice to me, she was trying to get me to do her dirty work.

"We can get the pizza to go. I'll walk you home and we can eat it on the way. You're getting bored here anyway, aren't you? Wouldn't you rather be home, watching TV?"

She wasn't expecting me to answer. She was just telling me what she expected me to do.

I didn't want to ask Eddy for pizza because, even as a kid, I was aware of how things worked. If he gave me something, then he would want something from me. If he was nice to me, I would be expected to be nice to him. Up to that point, I had felt reasonably comfortable with Eddy. However, I feared asking him for something he hadn't offered me.

I was between a rock and a hard place. If I didn't go along with Sharon, she would be mad at me. Would she be mad enough to hit me or hurt me in some other way? I didn't know her well enough to predict her actions. If I asked Eddy, he would probably want something from me, too. I hadn't feared him up to this point, but he may try to touch me like other males in my life had done. I knew I had to make a decision: Choose someone's side and just bear the wrath of the other.

I decided to please Sharon. The threat of her anger was more immediate than Eddy's, so I did what I needed to do to keep myself safe in the moment. I told Eddy I was hungry, and I would really like a pizza. He hesitated but finally gave in.

When the pizza came, Sharon told Eddy I was bored, wanted to go home, and she would walk me back to their apartment. We left the bar and as we walked the seven blocks to their place, I ate some of the pizza, but Sharon had most of it. When we got there, it was all gone.

Sharon went straight back to the bar, and I was alone. I don't remember being scared, even though it was night and the trailer park was in a bad neighborhood. Being left alone was what I really wanted.

When other people were around, especially adults, I always worried about what they wanted me to do or what they would do to me. I always had to read people to figure out if they were happy, sad, or angry. Then I had to figure out how to maneuver myself to stay safe. It was exhausting for me to be around people. For me, being alone was safe and relaxing. I didn't need to worry about anyone else. Children often have a safe place where they go like a tree or playhouse. My safe place was being alone and watching TV. No one bothered me and I could be carried away to different places and other lives. For the few hours after Sharon left, I was in my safe place, alone with a TV. That soon changed.

Around 10 or 11 p.m. Eddy and Sharon came home. My wonderful quiet was broken. They were both drunk, having spent several hours at the bar. However, drunken adults were nothing new for me; they just were a part of my life. As I sat in the dark living room, with the only light coming from the TV, I tried to become invisible. I lay down on the couch to hide. I said nothing and prayed they would forget I was there.

They were angry with each other, so the tension was high. They weren't violent; they weren't beating each other up and I was thankful for that. Sharon went to their bedroom, and Eddy came and sat on the couch with me. It made me nervous that he was sitting there beside me in the dark. I hadn't really been afraid of Eddy before, but I was then. Being alone with a man in the dark meant only one thing to me. And I was right.

"Come and sit on my lap," he said as he patted the top of his thighs. This was the payback for the pizza. He had been nice to me; now I had to be nice to him. I looked at him knowing I had no choice. I sat on his lap. My fears of abuse came true as he moved his hand up my leg and under my shorts. He started touching my private parts, and I jumped up off his lap and ran to the small bed in the corner of the room where I was supposed to sleep.

I prayed that he wouldn't come over to me. I lay there, terrified, trying to tune out every other sound in the house so I could hear only him. I listened as hard as I could for his footsteps and his breathing. I felt trapped. Anything might happen, and I couldn't control it. Fear gripped my entire body, and I tried to be quiet as my breathing came hard and fast. Even though it was summer and there wasn't air conditioning in the house, I pulled the covers over me. They offered a barrier of protection that helped me feel invisible.

Then I heard him get off the couch and walk into his and Sharon's bedroom and close the door. For the moment I felt safe. I wanted to leave, to run out of the house, but I had no place to go. So I tried to stay awake all night. After a while I heard snoring coming from their room, and I felt a little safer and finally went to sleep.

I don't remember much about the next day until the evening came. Being outside, away from Eddy, felt safer to me, so I stayed outside all day. Eddy and Sharon didn't seem to care what I was doing. But then evening came, and the darkness of night fell. No one called me into the house, and eventually the lights went out. After that, I had to make a decision; should I go back into the dark house or stay outside? Again I decided to do what would keep me safe in that moment. If there were dangers outside, I knew I could run away. But if I went back into the house, I would be trapped, like I had been the night before. I was sure tonight I would not be as lucky. So I made my decision: I stayed outside.

My first thought was to go into our trailer. I would be safe in there, wouldn't I? So I went inside the dark trailer. Turning on the lights was not an option. Eddy might see them and come after me. But the longer I stayed in there, the more frightened I became. This would be the first place he would look for me. Even if I locked the door, he could still come in because he was the manager and had keys to all the trailers. There was only one door out of the trailer, so if he came in, I would be trapped.

I went out of the trailer and walked around the block. One of the neighbors across the street was sitting on her front porch, so I crossed the street and walked on that side of the block. She was an older woman, and I had never really had any contact with her, but I had no reason to fear her either. Maybe she could help me. She was drinking a bottle of Coke, and I was hoping she would offer me one. I walked by her house and around the whole block several times, passing her with each rotation. It seemed like a long time to me, but it was probably only the second or third time around when the lady asked me, "What are you doing? You're out here kind of late all by yourself."

"Well, I'm supposed to stay with Eddy and Sharon," I

said, pointing to their apartment. "My mom is out of town, and they're taking care of me. But their lights are out, and I don't want to wake them up by going back inside the house." As I said this, I was looking at the bottle of Coke in her hand. It was watery on the outside, so I could tell it was cold.

She saw me looking at her bottle and finally said, "Do you want a bottle of pop?"

"Sure," I said, a smile widening on my face.

"Come sit on the porch, and I'll get you one." She walked into her house and soon returned with a cold bottle in her hand. She had already taken off the cap, so when she handed it to me, I started drinking.

We sat on her porch talking for a while. She asked about school and what grade I was in. When she asked who my mother was, I told her, and she got a disgusted look on her face and said, "Oh, her."

After a while, she stood up, "Well, it's time for me to go to bed. Are you going to stay out here all night or are you going to go back and stay with them?"

"Well, I really don't want to wake them up. They're probably asleep because the lights are all out. If I wake them up, they might get mad at me."

"You can sleep on my couch if you like. Just for tonight."

"Okay," I said, relieved that I would have a place to sleep that night. Inside I saw nothing fancy, just an old house with a couch, chair, and TV in the living room. She brought me a sheet and pillow to put on the couch.

"Take your shoes off. I don't want you to put your shoes on my clean sheet."

I took my shoes off and lay down on the couch. She said good night and turned off the light.

Amazingly, I felt safe staying with this stranger and sleeping on her couch. I knew I would be away from Eddy, and that was all the safety I needed for that night.

I am thankful to this woman, but I also consider this to be one of the most difficult but bravest decisions I ever made. I did what I needed to do to keep myself safe. Even as a child, I could make decisions that would change the rest of my life.

This decision did just that. The kind neighbor called the child welfare authorities. That call started the process of removing me from the home.

Chapter 17
Leaving My Life

July 10, 1970
"Katherine Shorny is found to be a neglected child."
Court Record, The State of Nebraska

Josephine came back on Sunday evening. Things were strained between Eddy, Sharon, and me. They didn't question where I had been the night before. Maybe they were afraid that if they got mad at me for not coming home, I would tell Josephine what Eddy had done to me. I don't know why their children had been taken away from them, but maybe Eddy feared he would be arrested for child sexual abuse.

What Eddy and Sharon didn't know is that I wasn't going to tell my mom what happened. For me, this kind of stuff happened to girls. This was how all men were, what they wanted. Besides, what would or could my mother do? She might get all mad and offended, but in the end she was powerless to take care of herself, let alone me. She would never call the cops. They were the enemy, not her friends. Plus, she wouldn't have had the courage to rat out her friends. This was her community, her tribe. They were the ones who fed her addictions and with whom she felt accepted. I truly believe she wanted to take care of me, but she had no way to do that.

On Monday, Josephine and I were at Eddy and Sharon's apartment. The adults were talking, and I sat with them.

"Who is that at your trailer, Jody?" Eddy asked as he looked out the window.

We all looked out the window.

"I don't know. I don't know anyone with a car like that," Josephine said. It was a newer-model white car. It wasn't a cool car, like a '57 Chevy or a '65 Mustang, so I had no idea what kind it was.

"Oh, shit! I know who that is," Sharon said as we saw the person walking toward their apartment. "That's ole lady Roper."

"Jody, take Kathy into the bedroom, shut the door, and be quiet. We'll take care of this." Eddy said.

So Josephine and I quickly went into the back bedroom and shut the door. We heard the knock, and Eddy answered, but we couldn't hear what they were saying. After a while, Sharon opened the door and said we could come out.

"Who was that?" Josephine asked when we were back in the living room.

"That was Roper," Eddy said.

"She's the welfare bitch that took our kids away," Sharon said.

"But what does she want with me? Why would she want to take Kathy away?" Josephine asked.

I looked down at my shoes, but I'm sure Eddy and Sharon were looking at each other.

"Somebody probably reported you as an unfit mother because of all the drinking, bars, and men you hang out with," said Eddy.

"That's probably it. If you just lay off the booze and men for a while, she'll leave you alone," said Sharon.

Josephine believed what they said and put the fault for Roper's visit on herself. However, the reality is that children are not taken away because of a mother's drinking and promiscuity. Her biggest mistake was that she had left me in Eddie and Sharon's care. They blamed her because they were really the ones at fault.

Mrs. Roper came to our trailer because I had stayed with the kind neighbor that night. That neighbor was the one who called. I stayed with her because I was too afraid to go back to Eddy and Sharon's house. I was afraid Eddy would molest or rape me like he had tried the night before. They put the blame on Josephine to get it off themselves.

Even though I knew the truth about what had happened that weekend, I believed their lie, just like Josephine did. I believed that her alcoholism and promiscuity had caused my removal from the home. After I was taken away, I always thought she wasn't able to stay away from the bars and men in order to keep me. I thought she had chosen that life over me and that's why I was taken away. I believed she didn't love me enough to change. This added to my sense of worthlessness. If my mother didn't love me enough to change her lifestyle to keep me, how could anyone else love me?

Not until writing this book and reexamining this story did I grasp that Eddy and Sharon said these things to Josephine to cover up their wrongdoing. They weren't trying to help Josephine keep me with their sage advice; they were trying to keep themselves from a possible conviction of child sexual abuse.

"Maybe it would be good for Kathy to go away for a while," Eddy said.

"Go away? What do you mean?" Josephine asked.

"Well, ole lady Roper isn't going to stop. She'll be back again tomorrow to try and take Kathy. We know some people who live on the edge of town. She could go and stay with them, just until things cool off."

"But how long would she stay there?" Josephine asked.

"Probably not more than a week. You get your act cleaned up, stay away from the bars and men, and Roper will leave you alone."

"If you don't do this, ole lady Roper will be back tomorrow with the cops and search the place. We can't keep hiding her here," Sharon said.

Josephine agreed. She went to our trailer and got some of my stuff. Then Eddy and Sharon put a blanket around me and walked me to their car. They were trying to hide me in case Mrs. Roper was still around. I lay down in the backseat.

Josephine got in beside me, and Eddy and Sharon were in the front. We drove out of downtown Lincoln and to the house of these "friends."

The woman wasn't surprised when she saw us at the door. We all went into the house, sat down, and talked a little. Either Eddy or Sharon must have called her before we left because she seemed to know what was going on. After a while, Josephine, Eddy, and Sharon got up to leave. I had stayed by my mom the whole time. She was the last little bit of security I had left in my life, but now that was leaving. I hugged her and just hung on; I didn't want to let go. Josephine tried to pull me off, "It will be okay, Katherine. You just stay with this lady for a few days, and then I'll come get you. Maybe we'll go see Aunt Dona, Debbie, and Steve when I come back."

The promise of seeing Dona and my cousins was a good way to get me to do things, but I still wasn't convinced. I hugged her tighter and begged, "Don't go."

Instead of pulling me away, Josephine started crying. Eddy stepped in. He pulled her back and separated us. I stepped back because I didn't want him to touch me.

"Come on, Jody, we've got to go," he said.

As they were walking out the door, the woman said to Eddy and Sharon, "I won't lie for her." Looking at my mother, she said, "If they come here, I'll let them take the girl."

I watched from the screen door as they walked down the sidewalk and out to the car. Little did I know it would be much longer than a week before I would see Josephine again. Thankfully, I would never again see Eddie and Sharon.

This whole situation was so bizarre. Who was this woman and why was she letting me stay with her? If the motive for this little caper was to protect Eddy from the police and not to keep me safe, then this woman may have been a relative of Eddy's or Sharon's. She may have been helping them and not my mother.

Whoever she was, she was nice and not at all like Josephine, Sharon, or Eddy. She seemed to be a good person who wasn't an alcoholic. Her house was small and old but also neat and clean, and she made good food. She did have a husband, but he was only there in the mornings and evenings. During the day, while we were at home, he was at work.

One nice thing I remember the woman doing for me was buying me training bras. I would be turning eleven in a couple months. My body was starting to change from that of a girl to a young woman. This lady recognized that, and she took me to K-Mart and bought me a couple of training bras.

Even though these people were nice, I still missed my mom and wondered when she would come back to get me. Being taken away from her was not something I wanted. I didn't like living with her because I never knew what she would do next or what would happen next. I wanted my situation to change, but I didn't want to be taken away from my mother.

However, that's what happened. The second or third day I was in hiding, I saw the police car pull up along with the white car we had seen at our trailer park. I knew immediately who it was and why she was there. It was the social worker,

Mrs. Roper, and she had come to take me away. To say I was scared would be an understatement. I was terrified of the unknown, of not knowing what was coming or how to respond. I had always been able to have some control. I had learned how to read people and knew how to act so I would be safe. But here I didn't know where I was going or what the rules would be. I didn't feel like I would have any control, and that scared me.

When Mrs. Roper knocked on the door, the woman I was staying with said, "Get your things. It's time to go." I did not resist; I knew there was no resisting anymore. The woman and Mrs. Roper talked a little at the door, but it was just an unnecessary formality. We all knew why she had come. She introduced herself to me, but I could not speak. It took every bit of strength I had to contain the ocean of tears welling up in my body. I didn't want to go. I didn't want to be without my mother and my brother. Would I ever see them again? And what about the rest of my family—Aunt Dona and my cousins? Would I ever see them again? My life was falling apart.

To make matters worse, during this most horrible time in my life, I was alone with strangers. There was no one I knew to comfort me, to tell me it would be okay. I was being taken away from my mother, but she wasn't even there to say goodbye. She wasn't a good mother by most people's standards, but she was my mother. She had cared for me when I was sick, given me gifts on birthdays and holidays. She was never violently mean to me, and I had always felt loved by her. But now, when I needed her the most, she wasn't there. I didn't know where she was or if I would ever see her again.

I took what few things I had and walked out the door on a hot summer's day. I got into a strange car, feeling like I was heading to a strange world. As we drove away, I felt like I was in a weird fog. I had to brace myself for what was coming, but I didn't know what that was, so how could I prepare myself?

As we drove, Mrs. Roper said she needed to stop at her house and check on something she had in the Crock-Pot. The house we stopped at was a lovely, small, one-story house with red shutters and gray roof. It also had beautiful green grass and small bushes planted close to the house. It was not big or fancy; it was just normal. It was exactly what I wanted for myself and my family. I wanted a normal life where I was doing normal things like checking on supper in the middle of the day.

I'm sure Mrs. Roper talked to me during the drive, but I have no memory of this. If she asked me any questions, I'm sure I nodded and smiled. I knew how to please her too. But I was so scared and sad I couldn't talk, let alone carry on a conversation.

We arrived at Cedars Children's Home. It was a large, two-story, brick building with beautiful green bushes and orange flowers in front. It looked nice but I felt like I was going into a prison. I knew I would be trapped there, not able to go where I wanted when I wanted. I would be forced to follow their rules and schedules, whatever those may be. There would be no more watching TV as long as I wanted to at night nor eating whatever was in fridge. No, this would be much, much different from what I was used to. I didn't know what this world held for me. I just knew I would lose a lot of the freedom I had had with my mother.

Yet it was also kind of nice. The building inside was beautiful compared to anything I had ever lived in. It had shiny, tiled floors, and painted walls. The walls were a light orange, not all white like a hospital, jail or doctor's office. As we walked down the halls, I smelled delicious food cooking. There would be good food here, a safe place to stay, and it was clean.

Maybe I would be safer and wouldn't have to worry about people hurting me or wonder if I would have enough to eat. Seeing this place and meeting some of the people helped me feel a little less terrified. I knew there was nothing I could do about it, so I had to make the best of it.

Chapter 18
Cedars Children's Home

When I first got to Cedars, I was scared. I really missed the mother part of Josephine. However, I felt relief because I wasn't around the alcoholic Josephine and the men in her life.

The staff and other children at Cedars were strangers to me. I didn't imagine they cared for me. Neither did I know the rules or expectations of this place. This meant I wasn't sure how to keep myself safe. Even though this was a safer place than I had ever been in, I didn't know that. I couldn't trust them simply because they were adults.

I was placed in the section of the home for girls my age and younger. We were all pretty equal, children of the same gender who had experienced some kind of trauma. And we were all there because we had no one to take care of us. But even with all these equalizers some girls tried to take control and sought power.

Every day after lunch we had to go to the bedroom to rest and have quiet time. The adult caretakers were not in the room at this time. We were by ourselves, and this is when some of the girls tried to show how powerful they could be. There were just two of them, as I remember. They went from bed to bed and asked each girl some dumb question. If you answered the question in a certain way you were okay, and they left you alone. If you answered it the wrong way, they hit you on your backside with a skinny little belt.

It was mean and unkind but probably benign compared to what most of us had been through. The girls doing this to us had probably been treated much worse. This was their attempt at power, their way of taking back some of the control they had lost. This mean stunt didn't really affect me because the girls meant nothing to me. Truthfully, the trauma I had suffered had been so much greater than what they were doing that their actions had little effect on my emotions.

Besides, I knew the way to survive was not to seek power over children. Children didn't matter; the fact that we were all at Cedars with no one to take care of us proved that. I knew the way to survive was to please older people. If you were charming, you had a better chance of manipulating the situation to keep yourself safe. If adults liked you, they were much less likely to hurt you. So I was nice and sided with everyone. I figured out what they wanted and tried to do that.

My strategy worked well. The first housemother at Cedars liked me so much she gave me a leather jumper that came in with some clothing donations. Leather clothes were popular in the late '60s and early '70s, so to have this come in on a clothing donation was unusual. When Fawn, the housemother, gave the jumper to me, I was so happy. Most of the clothes I had had up to this point were the hand-me-downs of hand-me-downs, items retrieved at clothes pantries or thrift stores. I was so happy to have it, even though I knew most of the other girls were jealous.

Fawn was the housemother for the first couple of months I was there. She was an older lady who lived in the apartment at the end of our hall, but she was just there during the week. On the weekends another woman came.

One weekend I got to go home with Fawn for a visit. And it was fun. There was a man at her house while I was there. I don't know if it was her boyfriend, husband, or brother. I saw nothing sexual going on, but they may have been behaving appropriately around me and keeping their sexual activities quiet. I had not been around many adults like that.

I don't know why Fawn took me home with her that weekend. Maybe it was just because she liked me. Maybe she felt sorry for me because I never got to go home or with other families on the weekends although I did go to Dona's house once or twice. Maybe she was thinking about becoming a foster parent and was taking me out for a test drive. If that were true, she must not have liked what she saw because she did not ask me to come live with her.

My ability to charm also came in handy at camp. Children at Cedars got to go to YMCA camp, and it was a lot of fun. We did all the usual camp stuff: arts and crafts, games, hiking, eating, and swimming. I learned how to swim that week. I was finally able to do normal things that kids would do.

At the end of the week, our counselor passed out various awards: Best Swimmer, Most Artistic, and stuff like that. Mine was for Cabin Sweetheart. I was so happy to get that title. I kept that award for many years. It meant a lot to me because that week at camp was probably one of the first times in my life that I really felt like a kid. For that week I belonged to this group. We had a lot of fun, and this award meant that they liked me.

The sense of belonging I felt at camp was not something I felt at the Cedars. It was not anything they did wrong, but I don't think any of us could feel like we belonged there. The reality was that it was just a holding tank. Everybody wanted to be somewhere else, not because it was a bad place but because it wasn't home. Most of the children were waiting, hoping to go back to their homes, back to their parents.

I remember two sisters who were there together, one in our section and one with the older girls. One Sunday afternoon the older sister came running down our hall. Before she said anything, you could see excitement filling every inch of her body. When she found her sister, she ran up and twirled her around. "Mom and Dad are coming. They're coming soon. Quick, go and get ready."

Because it was Sunday afternoon, we knew they were not going for a weekend visit, which would have started on Friday. If they were going home for good, the older sister would have said that and they'd be packing their things. No, we all knew they were going for a short visit, maybe just out for ice cream or maybe even to their house for supper. Whatever the situation was, those of us left behind felt jealous of them and sad for ourselves. This also made it clear that we were not a family at the children's home. Our true families were out there. We were all waiting, hoping they would come back and rescue us.

I felt this too, but I was also aware of the dangers in my home, and I didn't want to go back to those dangers. I didn't have much confidence that Josephine would ever be strong enough to do what she needed to do to get me back. Pat seemed out of the picture by then. He was back in Lincoln, but I don't think he ever came to see me while I was living in the home. I knew going to live with him would be dangerous as well.

A couple of times I went to Dona's for the weekend. Living with her family would have been my first choice, but I knew her life was full. She had four children already, plus she was getting a divorce from Arcy, her carnival-traveling husband.

Because I felt little hope for my future, I often cried myself to sleep. I didn't want to cry in front of the other girls. I was afraid they would make fun of me, see me as weak, and use me as a bully target. But in the dark and quiet of my lower bunk I let the tears flow quietly as I thought about all I had lost in a year and a half. Nobody wanted me. I knew Pat and Josephine loved me, but they didn't want me. I cried because I had no idea what the future held.

The one thing I should have gotten in the children's home but didn't was therapy. The only thing that resembled therapy was a visit with my social worker. She took me to a private room where I told her my story. This was the first and only time I was allowed to tell it. Sitting beside her on a couch, I poured out the whole tragic mess. How much I missed Frank and Pat. How much I hated the men Josephine was involved with and all her drinking, but how I missed her, too. How I wished she would change and be different. Through the words, I cried and cried.

I needed to tell this story many more times with a therapist. I needed a healthy adult who could help me understand what I was going through. However, I got only one therapy session to process the grief that I experienced. It would have to be enough to prepare me for moving into the next chapter in my life.

This next chapter of my life was already being prepared. Although I didn't know it, God was working in my life, preparing a place for me. God was working in the hearts and minds of a couple in Milford, Nebraska, giving them the desire and longing to take in a child. They masked this in practical terms; they needed a girl to help with the housework and the cleaning. But if this was their only wish, they could have hired someone for that. No, God was tugging at their hearts, planting the seed that would become my hope and salvation.

Chapter 19
They Wanted a Little Girl

In the fall of 1970, I started fifth grade at Park Elementary in Lincoln. All the elementary children at Cedars got on the bus each morning and headed off to school. Mr. Frobel was my teacher. He was nice, not anything special in my life but a good person.

One warm fall day as I got off the bus at Cedars and was ready to relax, the director, Alberta, called me into her office where two people were sitting. I wondered why they were there and who they were.

"This is Mr. and Mrs. Burkey," Alberta said.

Mr. Burkey held out his hand first, and I shook it; then I shook Mrs. Burkey's hand. I nodded and said hello, but I felt shy. Why were these people here I wondered? What did they want? I didn't know how to act, so I was quiet.

"How was school today?" Mr. Burkey asked.

"It was fine," I replied.

"What grade are you in?" Mrs. Burkey asked.

"The fifth grade. Mr. Frobel is my teacher."

"Do you like school?" Mr. Burkey asked.

"Oh yes. I like school," I said, trying to sound excited. I knew adults wanted children to enjoy school.

We talked for about half an hour about my school, the children's home, and their farm.

Alberta had left the room, and when she came back in, she asked if I would like to show them my room and the rest of the building. I agreed, and we went on a tour of the place.

Because I was feeling more comfortable now at Cedars, I knew my way around and could explain most things to them. After I showed them everything, we ended up at the front door.

"I guess we're ready to go," Mr. Burkey said.

"We were wondering if you would like to come and visit us for a weekend?" Mrs. Burkey asked.

"Sure," I said. "That would be fun." I was starting to feel relaxed and comfortable with these people. They seemed kind rather than scary, plus they were clean and didn't smell of cigarette smoke or alcohol. The thought of visiting them on their farm sounded like fun.

"We'll call back and talk to Alberta about when we could do that, " said Mr. Burkey.

Alberta nodded, and we all said goodbye.

I went back to my room, but I didn't fully realize what had just happened. How could I have known that this one day would mark a huge turning point in my life? How could I have known that all the things I so wanted in my life would start on this day? It seemed to be such an ordinary day. How could I have known that when I came back, waiting for me in Alberta's office was my miracle?

This revelation did not come to me on that day. These new people were nice, but I didn't think much about their visit. Other girls from the home had invited me to go with them on weekend visits. I assumed people from the community just

Floyd and Erma Burkey and Kathy, December 1970

did this to be nice to the poor, unfortunate children without families. I had no idea the Burkeys would be a possible family for me. I was still thinking I would go back to live with Josephine or maybe Dona.

My first visit to Milford was in early October. The Burkeys came on a Friday afternoon. I had gotten home from school and packed a few things when the housemother said they were here. This weekend I was the one who got to go somewhere. It wasn't my home, but I was going to a home, an actual house where a family lived.

I gathered my stuff and ran down the stairs. They were waiting at the front door, and I got in their car. I was my usual charming, sweetheart self. This was not an act; this was just the way I knew I needed to behave around people. I didn't know these people at all; they were strangers. My instincts told me they were okay, but I wasn't sure. I knew I needed to make them feel happy so hopefully I could be safe.

The drive from Lincoln to Milford was not long. As we left the children's home, we drove through parts of Lincoln I did not recognize. But then we came to familiar territory. No one was talking, and I was glad for that because my happy exterior melted away as I saw familiar places. Tears filled my eyes. I stared out the window. I tried to hold the tears back. I didn't want the people in front to see me crying. They might think I didn't like them or that I didn't want to go with them and that might make them mad at me. I didn't know what they would do to me if they were mad.

My throat got thicker and my chest heavy. I saw places I had gone to with Pat and Josephine. I saw the bar where Josephine and Marvin had first coaxed me to sing "Harper Valley PTA." There was the rescue mission where we had stayed when we moved back from Ulysses. I saw bars and stores that only a few months ago I had been in with Pat and Josephine. Now all that had changed. I stared out the window. Maybe I would see my brother and mother coming out of one of the bars or walking down the street. I realized how much I missed them.

As we turned off Ninth Street onto O and drove west over the huge viaduct, I felt the biggest grief of all. Under the viaduct was the huge scrap metal business where Frank took our family when he sold the metal he had picked up at dumps. There were the scales where we drove our car to be weighed. I wanted to look away but couldn't. This place represented a positive part of my childhood. As long as I could, I strained to see the junkyard, but finally it was gone from my view. My family was gone too, and the pain I felt as I sat quietly crying in the backseat with these strangers nearly tore my little body apart. I had lost my whole family. They weren't a great family, but they were my family. I would never have them back. I had no idea what would happen next in my life. Where would I go? Who would care for me?

I strained to see the junkyard as long as I could, but finally it was gone. So I turned and looked forward as we drove west toward Milford.

We got to Milford and stopped at a small café on Main

Street. A few tables and a long counter with stools filled most of the space. We sat at the counter and ordered. I got a hamburger, fries, and a Coke. Mr. and Mrs. Burkey were nice and let me have whatever I wanted.

What I really wanted I had seen when I first walked into the café. At the end of the counter was a cake stand covered with glass. Inside was a chocolate cake. A couple of pieces had already been taken out, so I could see the middle of the cake. It was round with two chocolate layers that I was sure would be delicious. Between the layers and covering the entire outside was creamy, smooth chocolate frosting. Mr. Burkey saw me looking at the cake and asked if I wanted a piece. "Oh yes," I answered. The sheer joy at the thought of having this cake caused me to let my guard down for a moment. I liked many, many foods, but cake, especially chocolate cake, was my favorite. After having such a good meal of a hamburger and fries, to have cake on top of it made me realize that having enough food would not be an issue here. That was good. However, if I let my guard down too much, if I said the wrong thing, they might get mad at me. I wanted to make sure they were happy with me. What I didn't realize as a young child was that making me happy made them happy. I don't think I had ever experienced that before with the adults in my life.

The rest of the weekend went fine. I began calling them by their names, Erma and Floyd. They did some stuff with me, but I had a lot of time on my own. I played with their big, beautiful dog. I helped Erma with cleaning the house and cooking the food. I enjoyed that, too. Then on Sunday, after church, they took me back to Cedars. They said they would see me again.

The next weekend I went for a visit to the Burkeys and took one of the other girls from the home. Sandy had taken me on a visit with her one weekend, so now it was my turn to return the favor.

It was fun having someone else along. We played outside together and explored the farm. But that whole weekend I was also scared. What if they really did want to have a child come and live with them? What if they had decided on me first, but now that they saw Sandy, maybe they liked her better? Maybe spending the weekend with her would make them realize that they didn't want me. Sandy wasn't prettier or smarter than I was, but she seemed to be able to talk with them more easily. Especially Mr. Burkey, Floyd. Sandy always got up quicker than me when Erma needed something done. Why would they choose me over Sandy? Why would anyone really want me? If my own mother didn't love me enough to keep me, why would anyone else want me?

As this fear and sadness consumed me, the weekend was no longer about having fun on the farm. Now it was about competing with Sandy. It was about being the smartest, the prettiest, the most helpful, and always saying the right thing, so they would choose me instead of her.

I worried about this after the weekend visit was over. What if they asked Sandy to visit them again and not me? If that happened, then I knew there would be no hope for me to live with them. Then who would want me? I would have liked to live with Dona and her family, but she had never asked me if I wanted to come. All these people I thought loved me were not there now. I guess they didn't want me either.

My load of worry and fear was lifted when Alberta said the Burkeys wanted me to come for another visit. Oh, thank you, God, I thought. They didn't want Sandy. They wanted me. I went again to their farm the next weekend. After a full day of playing, riding in the tractor, helping make supper, and cleaning up, I sat in the bedroom I had been sleeping in for the last three visits. I had just taken a bath and had on clean, soft pajamas. I loved this room. It was huge. There were two beds in it because Janet and Loree, the Burkeys' oldest and youngest daughters, now grown and living on their own, had slept there. It had a beautiful red carpet, and the room was clean and organized. I could still smell the lingering aroma of supper—fried chicken and mashed potatoes.

The bedroom closet was tidy and clean. It was nearly empty with just a couple of blankets. I walked into the closet and ran my hand on each of the white, painted shelves. If I lived here, I thought, I would put my shirts on this shelf and my pants here. In my mind, I arranged all my clothes and other belongings on these shelves. I imagined all the ways I would arrange not only the closet, but the whole room.

I went back, sat on the bed, and realized it was only a dream. Coming from my life to this life would be like jumping across the Grand Canyon. Impossible, I thought. I could hope and dream all I wanted, but living in this house with this family would never happen. Things this good didn't happen to me.

The next day, after church we ate at a restaurant for lunch. Then we went back to their house so I could pack my stuff up and go back to Cedars. This had become routine. When I had my things packed up and was ready to leave, they asked me to sit at the table. They had something they wanted to talk about.

Floyd spoke first, "We wanted to talk to you about coming out here on the weekends."

Oh no, I thought. They're tired of me. They don't want me to come out anymore. I knew this was too good to be true. I knew it would never last.

"Well, we were wondering," he continued, "if you would like to come and live with us here on the farm?"

I was quiet for a little while because I couldn't believe what they were saying.

When I didn't respond, Erma spoke up. "Well, is that something you think you might like?"

I couldn't believe what they were asking me. Of course, I wanted to live here with them. But as I thought a little more, I wondered what this really meant. Who would be my family if I lived with them? What about Aunt Dona, Steve and Debbie? Would I ever see them again?

So my first response was, "I think my Aunt Dona wants me to come and live with her."

"Well, the social worker said that wasn't going to work out. But you can come and live with us if you want," Floyd said.

Until that moment, I hadn't truly realized the possibility of living with Aunt Dona was gone. That door closing made me sad. But this door opening seemed really good. These people were nice to me.

"Okay, that sounds good," I finally said. I looked from one to the other, and they were both smiling at me.

"Well, good. We'll tell the social worker. It will probably be a couple of weeks, but the next time you come, it should be to live with us," Floyd said.

As we drove back to Lincoln, my mind was filled with this new possibility. As the miles passed, I got more and more excited. When I got out of the car at Cedars, I was very excited.

"So I'm really going to come and live with you?"

"We think so," Erma said, "if everything works out."

I gave them a big smile and hugged each of them. As I turned and walked into the building, I felt happier than I had ever been.

Chapter 20
My New Life

On Wednesday afternoon, before the Thanksgiving weekend of 1970, I walked out of Cedars Home for Children for the last time. I was going to have a family and a home again. The waiting was over.

It had been almost five months since I came to Cedars on that horrible, scary day. I'd become used to the routine, the people, and the other children. In a way, it was good I went there before going to live with the Burkeys. Living at Cedars for five months helped settle me down. I had become a pretty wild child living with Josephine and Pat. During those last few months with them, I had started smoking and did whatever I wanted to do.

For my confirmation at St. Mary's Catholic Church that spring, I was given a white Bible and white rosary. I put them in my top dresser drawer. The Bible and rosary lay there beside my pack of cigarettes. These items represented the two paths my life could take. Would I continue the legacy I was born with and live a life like Josephine? Or would I be able to break away and go down a new path?

Being at Cedars had helped settle me down and promised to help me find a new path for my life. Some routines were taking shape for me. There were consistent times to eat, go to bed, and get up. I was developing a sense of responsibility. Part of that was doing chores. Everyone at the children's home had various chores to do. We were not only expected to be accountable for ourselves, but also for helping maintain our living space. I had had no rules or consistency when I lived with Josephine. Now I had begun to learn many of these things for the first time. As I left Cedars, I was taking with me many new skills that would help me fit in better at my new home and make the transition a little easier.

Also, my physical health was better, and my brain was healthier. Cedars had helped calm my mind. No longer did I live in that crazy world of stress and chaos. I had safe, consistent adults around me. There were routines and things I could count on happening at the same time each day. This helped my brain calm down a little so it could function better. A child who lives with healthy adults often learns calming skills through their interactions with each other. I was beginning to learn some of these skills at Cedars.

When Floyd and Erma pulled up in front of the home, I was packed and ready to go. As we drove away, I felt excited about this new chapter in my life. Driving through the streets of Lincoln wasn't nearly as difficult as it had been that first time. I still looked at the familiar places and I felt sad, but the intense pain was not there, and the tears did not come.

When we got to the farm, we ate supper. Then we talked about what would happen the next day. After getting up early, we'd drive in the car for several hours to Kansas to share Thanksgiving with the Burkey children and their famlies. We'd go to the home of their oldest daughter, Janet.

She and her husband, Stan, lived on a farm with their three children, Marty, Jody and Cindy. The other Burkey children would also be there: John and his new wife, Brenda; Paulene and her husband, Ray, plus their children, Shelly and Steve; as well as Loree, Floyd and Erma's youngest daughter.

I felt overwhelmed. I couldn't keep the names straight, especially since there were so many, and I knew none of the people. It all seemed unreal to me. Not unreal like the day Mrs. Roper came and took me to Cedars. That was a scary experience. No, this was a good unreal. I was scared but also excited. I didn't think these new people would be mean to me or be drinking and unpredictable. However, I really didn't know what to expect.

As I lay in bed that night, I felt lucky. Here I was in this beautiful house with two people who really seemed to care about me. Tomorrow I would get to go to Kansas and meet the rest of the family. I was very excited about going to another state. I had never been out of Nebraska.

I felt many conflicting and confusing emotions that night. I missed Josephine and Pat and wondered what they would be doing for Thanksgiving. However, I knew I did not want to go back and live with them. I did not want the life they were living. I wished they would change and provide a safe home for me. My real desire was to live with them, but I wanted them to be like Floyd and Erma.

I also loved this new life and wanted to be here. However, staying here would mean being whatever these people wanted me to be. To stay alive and safe meant staying with these people and in this family.

I also knew it was the Burkeys' choice that I was here, and it would be their choice to send me away. So I would do what I had always done; I'd do whatever it took to keep myself safe. I would be whoever they wanted me to be. If I did that well enough, maybe they would keep me. But I could only control what I could control, and that was to keep them happy so I would be safe.

Now I realize this was an unhealthy way for me to view life. But all children who suffer the trauma of abuse, neglect, and removal from their families have psychological issues to deal with on some level. My desire to focus on keeping my new parents happy and be whatever they wanted me to be may not have been a healthy attitude, but it served me well in the moment. I was able to fit in and mold myself to their life and their expectations. Fortunately, Floyd and Erma really did want the best for me.

This new journey would not be easy. There would be many bumps along the way. But this was my miracle. God had brought me here and given me this amazing gift of a new life. I wanted to make the most of this opportunity. Many people would help me along the way, not only this new family, but new friends as well. I was also about to get an amazing church family that would love and nurture me and also strengthen my faith and walk with God. Yes, tomorrow I was going to a different state to meet a new family, but I was also starting on a journey toward a new life.

Chapter 21
My New Family

"Okay, I think we've got everything," Floyd said as he shut the trunk of the green Dodge. Floyd, Erma, and I got into the car and headed for Hesston, Kansas, for Thanksgiving. As we drove out the long lane that led to the main road, gravel crackling under the tires, I realized that once again I was going to a new and strange place.

From the back seat I looked out the window at the cows in their pens. Even though I had only been to the farm on visits, the place was starting to feel familiar. And I felt safe with Erma and Floyd. I trusted they would not take me anywhere bad or where people would hurt me. Their presence softened my anxiety.

Looking out the window occupied my time for the first hour of travel. I asked repeatedly, "Are we out of Nebraska yet?" I was excited about the new adventure.

Finally, Floyd said, "Okay, we're in Kansas now." As I looked out the window, I was disappointed. Kansas looked a lot like Nebraska. I thought there would be something more exciting about passing from one state to another.

I went back to playing with the small Barbie doll I'd brought. Soon I fell asleep. The next thing I knew Erma was touching my shoulder, waking me gently and saying we had arrived at Janet and Stan's house.

I walked behind Floyd and Erma into the old farmhouse. The room was full of strangers. I suddenly became shy, but Floyd coaxed me out from behind him and introduced me to everyone. They all seemed nice. No one really scared me. I could smell cigarette smoke on a couple of the people, but no one smelled like alcohol. This was a comfort to me.

Soon everyone went back to visiting or watching TV. Most of the women went into the kitchen. I followed along. When I had done the few tasks I was able to do, like putting dishes on the table, Janet took me to another room and introduced me to the children of the family. She said I could play with them. Marty and Jody were the closest to my age, nine and six. Then there were the younger children: Cindy, Shelly, and Steve. They were three and four. I was glad to be with the kids. This was a place where I could relax and be myself. I didn't feel a need to please them like I did the adults.

When the weekend was over, we said our goodbyes, and Floyd, Erma, and I drove back to Nebraska.

The next big family celebration was Christmas. I was excited to see the children again. Christmas Day was fun, and I got wonderful gifts, new items that were actually bought and not from the thrift stores or the social worker. John and Brenda gave me a book titled *Blue Willow*. I also got a transistor radio and a knitting kit.

The whole family was there for about a week, and we had a lot of fun. Again I felt my safe place was being with the children. I even organized a little Christmas play that we put on. The skit was about a poor woman living in a box, and she was cold and hungry at Christmas. I was the poor homeless woman, and Marty and Jody brought me food and blankets.

It was simple, but looking back on it now, this was my way to express my sadness over missing Josephine. I wondered where she was this Christmas and what she and Pat were doing. It was also a way to express my wish to be able to help her. I don't remember having any communication with her that Christmas.

Kathy's first Christmas with the Burkeys, 1970

Being in this new family, I was already figuring out how to be accepted and to stay safe. I felt that talking about Josephine and how much I missed her would make this family feel I didn't want to be with them. So my need to express my grief came out in this simple Christmas play. I created my own form of self-therapy.

The Burkeys became my new family. They were kind and loving, but everything was not perfect. Floyd was a strong disciplinarian with a "spare the rod, spoil the child" attitude. He wanted to help children do the right thing. While his discipline was based in love, I found it difficult to handle at times. However, nothing is perfect in life, and having this family with their love, care, and protection was more than I ever thought possible. They were my miracle, and my life was starting on a new course.

I had many fun and loving times with Erma and Floyd. Erma and I worked together in the house and garden. We enjoyed cooking together. She taught me how to cook, and she even let me try new recipes. Working in the garden and raising our own food was fun as well. During the summer, at meal times we would compare the items we had raised to those we bought. This gave me a sense of accomplishment and pride to know I could help raise our food.

Erma and I also went shopping in Lincoln. This was always fun. It was such a wonderful experience buying new clothes rather than always getting them from a thrift store or clothing pantry.

I was not with Floyd as much because he was always outside doing the farm work. One day he needed help sorting cattle, and no one else was around. I went out to help him. I was in the pen with him, and my job was to open and close the gate. As the cows came through, most of them would go into another pen, but when he gave me the signal, he wanted me to close the gate so the cow would go into a chute and up into the truck. This system worked well for a while; most of the cows obediently went into the chute when I closed the gate. One cow had a different idea. Dad gave me the signal, and I closed the gate, but the cow kept coming towards me. Wanting to do a good job, I stood my ground and tried to not let the cow through. The cow won though; she pushed through the gate and I fell down hard.

That was the end of the sorting. Dad took me into the house to make sure I was okay. I was afraid he would be mad at me. But he said he was very proud of me and that I had tried to do a good job. He also warned me that trying to stand my ground with a cow was not a smart thing to do.

Dad was also a big kidder and loved to tease people, especially children. One summer night the girls from my Sunday school class came out for a slumber party. We decided it would be fun to sleep in the big farm trunk, the one we hauled grain in. It was parked in the metal machine shed close to the house. Dad said it would be okay to sleep in it if we first swept it out. This was a big job, and we worked a long time getting all the grain and dust out of it. Finally, we settled in with our sleeping bags and snacks Mom had made for us.

We were all laughing and talking when we heard something pound on the roof of the shed. The sound got louder and louder. We didn't know if it was hail or someone shooting a gun. Scared, we started screaming and we continued until we realized the noise had stopped. Then in the quiet we heard someone laughing and laughing. We went outside to see who it was and found my dad, still laughing, standing by the shed with a bucket half full of rocks beside him. He had been throwing rocks on the metal roof of the shed and that's what had made the horrible racket.

Milford school was also a good, safe place for me. I started at the elementary in the fifth grade. Mrs. Moser was my teacher. She was kind, and she didn't treat me different because I was a foster child. Rather she seemed to understand how difficult it was for me in this new situation and tried to help me feel accepted.

I stayed in the Milford school system until I graduated from high school. I had many friends and enjoyed my time there. However, the shadow of being a foster child stayed with me all through high school. I often felt like I was on the outside looking in. My class was small, only fifty-three students, so everyone knew I was a foster child. It probably made more of a difference to me than it did to any of the other students, but I always felt different.

Kathy at age 12
Milford Elementary School

To feel accepted, I tried to be like everyone else. I gravitated toward the good kids. This may have been because I didn't feel comfortable with people who resembled Pat and his friends. I was involved in school activities: choir, plays, and the pep club. I did well in school and was accepted into the National Honor Society my sophomore year.

The other great part of my life was the church. We attended Bellwood Mennonite in Milford. I was part of Sunday school and MYF (Mennonite Youth Fellowship). We did a lot of group things together and had parties, including slumber parties. There was also a group for the girls called GMSA (Girls Missionary Service Auxiliary) where we made crafts and sold them to raise money for overseas missions. Even though these were normal childhood activities for most, they were new to me. But I was thankful I could be a child. I also felt relaxed around the adults in the church. Not all the adults in the church paid attention to me, but the ones who did were kind and loving. The women in the church were people I wanted to model my life after, and I felt the men would protect me rather than abuse me. This was such a change from my life with Josephine. Feeling safe, protected, and cared about and having positive role models are important parts of a healthy childhood. I was finally getting that.

Bellwood Church was a place of love and acceptance for me, even more than in my new family. Even though my family was good to me and cared for me, I often felt like I was on the outside looking in, and I had to continually please them so they would keep me. They never said this to me, but I always feared they would send me back to Cedars if I displeased them and they decided they didn't want me anymore. At church, I felt truly loved and valued. Because of this I felt God's love for me in many ways. This provided the foundation of the strong faith I have today.

As for Josephine, she was jailed for ten days after I was taken to Cedars. She was not allowed to see me for a year. When she was able to visit me, she did not follow the rules the court had set up and came to the farm unannounced, sometimes with Pat and usually with several men. Floyd and Erma reported this to my social worker, and after that I was only able to have supervised visits at the social worker's office in Lincoln.

Pat and Josephine often called at Christmas. They were usually drunk when they called. It was difficult to see them or talk to them on the phone.

My life had been split in two, and I found it difficult straddling both sides. I still cared about Josephine and Pat, but I didn't want to go back to the life I had with them. My new family loved me, cared for me, and wanted the best for me. Gradually my loyalty shifted from Josephine and Pat to my new family.

In a way I had changed my identity. I pushed away my old life and tried to live fully in my new life. I hoped to push my past down so far that I would erase its existence.

After I graduated from high school, I went to Hesston College, a two-year small Mennonite college. It was located in Kansas and near where we had gone for that first Thanksgiving with the Burkeys. In that safe setting, I got a fresh start and changed my last name to Burkey. Whenever anyone asked where I was from, I usually said I grew up on a farm in Nebraska. I talked about Lincoln and my biological family only with my closest friends. Over the years I had sort of kept in touch with Josephine and Pat, but by the time I was a sophomore at Hesston, all communication with them ended.

One night in December 1979 I was home from Hesston for Christmas break. I got a phone call from Josephine, and she was drunk. During the conversation she asked me if I wanted to call her latest husband "Marvin" or "Daddy Marvin" (They stayed together for several years.) I was frustrated and outraged by this question. I had moved on in my life. I

Floyd and Erma Burkey

was a completely different person from the little girl she had left. I had done so much with my life, but she couldn't see any of it. Alcohol continued to control her. When she asked me this idiotic question, one she had asked many times before, I had finally had enough. I stood my ground with her and said, "I have someone here I call Dad."

"Do you consider them your parents more than me?" she asked.

"Yes I do," I answered. Then I started shaking and crying. I don't remember what her response was. I just stood there and cried.

My dad, Floyd, who was sitting in his recliner in the living room, listening and watching, came over to me and took the phone from my hand. He hung it up and engulfed me in a hug. I cried in his arms. A line had been crossed that day, and I would never go back. I had chosen my foster family over my biological one. At that point all contact with Josephine and Pat stopped.

After Hesston, I continued my education at Bethel College in North Newton, Kansas, receiving a bachelor's degree in elementary education. After a year in Mennonite voluntary service in St. Louis, I moved back to Kansas where I met Tim Wiens at Church of the Servant, a Mennonite congregation in Wichita. We were married in October of 1985. In this relationship I felt safe enough to start looking at my past. The first time I saw a therapist was at the Kansas University Medical Center in Wichita where Tim was in residency. I continue with therapy off and on, as issues come up from my childhood.

In 1991 Pat's wife called my mom, Erma, to tell her Josephine had cervical cancer and was not expected to live long. Pat's wife called the Burkeys because my biological family did not know where I was.

Tim and I, along with our daughters, Terra, age three, and Ruth, nine months, went to Nebraska. Terra and Ruth stayed with my mom and dad in Milford, and Tim and I went to Lincoln. We went to Josephine's small apartment in downtown Lincoln. Pat and Dona were also there.

We visited for a couple of hours. Tim asked a lot of good questions for me. I felt numb during the visit. My main emotion was fear. I was afraid Pat and Josephine would find out where we lived. I was afraid they would find out Tim was a doctor and try to get money from us. I really hoped Pat had changed, that he had also broken the cycle and was a safe person to have in my life and especially to have around my daughters. Sadly, from this visit I realized nothing had changed with either of them.

Right before Christmas we made the trip to Lincoln again. This time Josephine was in a nursing home. We took Terra and Ruth to meet her and got pictures of the four of us together. That was the last time I saw her.

Her funeral was in January 1992. I drove to Nebraska, and my mom Erma and I went to Josephine's funeral. It was at this funeral that I first met my aunt Della and aunt Gean, Josephine's two younger sisters.

After the funeral, my mom and I along with Pat, his wife, and Dona's children went to Dona's house. During this time Pat started talking about the girl he and his friends had raped. He laughed about it, saying how they had kicked her out of the car and left her naked in the street. This was when I fully realized he had not changed and was not a safe person for me to be with and especially not to have my daughters around. There was no way I would ever give him access to my children.

A few years after the funeral, I connected with Della and Gean. When I called Della and told her who I was, she said, "Oh, we've been wondering what happened to you." I visited her and Gean by myself one weekend. A couple of weeks later I took my family so they could learn to know my relatives. Della had her children and Gean's children come to her house to meet me. I got to meet many cousins, and this was a great afternoon.

Finally, I felt love and acceptance from my biological family. For years I had felt like no one from that family cared about me. But it was helpful to have them come and see me and want to get to know who I was. They wanted to know the little girl I had been. I could let her come out and not feel a need to hide her anymore. Also, this part of the family was more like me. They were not alcoholics. I don't remember any of them smoking. They were my biological family, and I felt safe with them.

That afternoon after we left Della's house, we drove back to Milford before going back to Kansas. Driving out to the farm felt like I was making a full circle. The first time I had come down this road, some thirty years earlier as an eleven-year-old, my life looked very different. In an effort to survive, I had tried to push away my old life and my biological family. I had been fairly successful, creating a new life for myself, but the past was always there and I had always feared it. But now my reconnection with part of that past had proven to be a good and healing experience.

I've learned that amid the pain, the abuse, the neglect, and the tragedy of my early home, snippets of hope and faith lifted me up. I'm grateful that they carried me away from a sad childhood of bars and dumps and into a God-filled adulthood of love and healthy relationships.

The Umbilical Cord

I wrote this poem when I was doing my healing work in therapy. I saw Josephine again before she died in 1990.

Our umbilical cord was connected that day.
Pain shot through my soul as they pulled it away.
They took me away as I trembled with fear.
So sad and so lonely, I wanted you near.

I love and I need you, oh, where did you go?
"Please tell me where is she? I just want to know.
You see, she's my mother and I'm alone here."
But no one would tell me; I shed only one tear.

The days turned to months and the months into years.
The umbilical cord weakened, and so did my fears.
I want to be with you, but not like before.
The men and the drinking I truly abhor.

The tie once between us turned empty and lame.
My love for you replaced with sadness and shame.
No longer did I want you attached to me.
That cord now was slashed, and I thought I was free.

For years now I've had some relief from the pain.
I've pushed it down, hoped it would not surface again.
But now you are old and you're dying alone.
I should come to you, let you see how I've grown.

You can't hurt me now; you're just someone I knew.
Dear dying old lady, I'm sorry for you.
I'm free of emotion and free of the pain.
Our tie now is gone, and I've made that quite plain.

But seeing you sober, I know it's not true.
You're still part of me, and I'm still part of you.
But so much is gone and so much is dying.
I realize that little girl is still crying.

Epilogue

The last piece of this story is Pat. As an adult, I often wondered if I should get in touch with him and try to help him. However, I knew I would never let him or any of his friends have access to my daughters. I didn't know how to connect with him in a safe way. I often sought counsel about this from friends and members in my small group at church. Their answers were always the same: Connecting with Pat didn't seem like a good thing to do. So I stayed away.

In January 2010, Dona called and said Pat had died. She didn't know many details. She had heard through friends of Pat that he died in a group home. She didn't know the cause of death. She put something in the paper, but no services were held. His ashes were at a funeral home in Lincoln.

I called the funeral home and asked who was picking up the ashes. They said no one had claimed them. They would keep the ashes for a couple of months, but if no one claimed them, they would be thrown in the trash. I decided to go to Lincoln and get his ashes.

When I got to Lincoln, Della went with me to the funeral home, and the funeral director sold me an urn in which he placed Pat's ashes. This is how I reconnected with my biological brother.

I brought his ashes to my home where the urn sits on a shelf in our living room. In a small way, having a part of my big brother here has encouraged me, even comforted me at times as I've written this book. I know I need to release his ashes and let him go. When this book is done, I plan to take his ashes to Nebraska and scatter them. I'll keep the urn I bought and use it as a planter. Putting something beautiful and living in his urn will help me remember the good and loving part of my brother.

July 2013

Acknowledgments

I would like to thank Laurie Oswald Robinson, author of *Forever Families* and editor at Mennonite Mission Network, for her wisdom and support. Laurie was my writing coach through this process. This book would not be in your hands today without the help of Laurie.

I would also like to thank my readers: Dr. Russell Fulmer from Emporia State University, Carol Hammond Paulsen Ph.D, Jeanette Harder Ph.D, Katherine Mick PhD. Their input helped greatly in making revisions and their encouragement of the story gave me the courage to continue the process.

My editors have also been a great help. Kara Schmidt was the first editor. Her gentle caring spirit helped me feel safe in letting her see my words and fix problems. Gordon Houser was also a great editor. His changes brought the book to life and made it much more reader friendly. June Galle Krehhiel helped me finished up the manuscript. She also made the manuscript more readable and her knowledge of the publishing journey has helped me get everything together and the book out the door.

The encouragement of my family and friends has also been very important. Special thanks goes to my husband Tim, whose faithful love, support and encouragement has helped me in many endeavors in my life and especially this one. My brother and sisters, and sister-in-law have also supported me in this journey. Also special thanks to my Aunt Dona. She was a constant help in my childhood and was always there for my biological family and our many needs.

About the Author

Katherine Burkey Wiens lives in Newton, Kansas with her husband Tim, a family practice physician. They have two daughters, Terra (and husband Das) and Ruth (and husband Matt). Kathy was an early childhood educator for 28 years, teaching both children and adults.

Kathy is a Licensed Professional Counselor and Trauma Recovery Coach. She holds graduate degree in Elementary Education from Wichita State University and Mental Health Counseling from Emporia State University. Kathy offers training and policy reviews to churches on child protection and sexual abuse prevention. Along with her work in churches she is Board Chair of Into Account, Witness Support Specialist for GRACE (Godly Response to Abuse in Christian Environments) and is on the list of speakers for Dove's Nest.

Kathy's new endeavor for 2020 is opening a Healing Art Studio in Marion, KS. The Studio will offer coaching, counseling and classes on health and wellness topics, as well as other forms of expressive arts.

Find out more by visiting katherinebwiens.com.

www.ingramcontent.com/pod-product-compliance
Lightning Source LLC
Chambersburg PA
CBHW060539100426
42743CB00009B/1573